THE BIBLE: God's Missionary Message to Man

Volume 2

Gilbert L. Guffin

The Church Study Course

Woman's Missionary Union
600 North Twentieth Street, Birmingham, Alabama 35203

This book is the text for course 3673 of Subject Area 36 (Missions) of the Church Study Course.

FOREWORD

We have traced in the Old Testament—from Genesis to Malachi—the unfolding of God's missionary message to man. We have seen how the divine promises to make a way of deliverance for fallen man date back to man's earliest experience. The amazing response of God's love to human need is to seek man even in his guilt. Adam hid from his Creator and deepened the gulf his disobedience had caused in his fellowship with God. But "God called unto Adam . . . Where art thou?" (Gen. 3:9).

In time, God chose Abraham (then called Abram) and made a "covenant" with him, that through his descendants all the nations of the earth should be blessed (Gen. 12:1-3), and that one should at last come of his "seed" through whom this promise would have its ultimate fulfilment (Gen. 17:5-8).

The Old Testament closes with the greatest seers of all time standing almost on tiptoe to see the *event* of the ages—the coming of God's Messiah. These "holy men of God [who] spake as they were moved by the Holy Ghost" (2 Peter 1:21) saw beyond the horizon of their times. What they beheld kept hope alive in Israel that God would one day do a work which would cause all men to marvel. As we turn the pages of the New Testament, it is with excitement that we hasten to see what that "marvel" really is.

As we open the New Testament, what do we discover? The answer may be familiar, but is it understood? We know the so-called Christmas story with which at least two of the Gospels begin—every detail—but have we pondered its significance to the missionary theme of the ages? to the mission of the church? to our mission personally?

The challenge for missionary concern continues to ring out. The deafening roar of our modern world revolution may tend to muffle the clarity of this challenge, but for the informed Christian this noise cannot entirely drown it out. What is the extent of man's response to God? More importantly, what is our own response personally? With these questions ringing in our ears we should humbly and prayerfully enter upon the study of the New Testament, resolved to see what it actually says about the missionary message of the ages.

If it were not so familiar, this would be the most exciting discovery ever made.

CONTENTS

II
Acts and the Epistles

1—Missions in the Purpose of His Coming

Matthew 1:1 to 3:17; Mark 1:1-11; Luke 1:1 to 3:23; John 1:1-18

"Yet . . . a little while . . . and the desire of all nations shall come: and . . . fill this house with glory," said Haggai centuries ago (Hag. 2:6-7). As the apostle Paul put it: "When the fulness of the time was come, God sent forth his Son, made of a woman, made under the law, to redeem them that were under the law, that we might receive the adoption of sons" (Gal. 4:4-5). But as the first chapters of each Gospel are examined, what can be found in them regarding the fulfilment of the prophecy and the Abrahamic Covenant? Is the thread of missionary concern traceable throughout the Old Testament discovered here? Or was it only discovered later by the church? To answer these questions calls for an examination of what is said about the coming of Christ in each Gospel.

The Purpose Proclaimed in Mark

As we turn to this Gospel, generally felt to be the first written, we come immediately upon a familiar (Malachi) prophecy: "Behold, I send my messenger before thy face, which shall prepare thy way before thee" (Mark 1:2). Mark applies this reference to John the Baptist and adds: "The voice of one crying in the wilderness, Prepare ye the way of the Lord, make his paths straight (Mark 1:3). The mission of John the Baptist was to prepare the way for the coming of the Messiah. John later preached: "There cometh one mightier than I after me, the latchet of whose shoes I am not worthy to stoop down and unloose" (Mark 1:7).

Though John had been baptizing men with water upon the evidence of their true repentance, he declared that the One who was shortly to come would baptize with the Holy Spirit.

Into this scene on the Jordan came Jesus of Nazareth who was later baptized by John. As Jesus came up and out of the water, the Holy Spirit "like a dove" descended upon him; and a voice out of heaven declared, "Thou art my beloved Son, in whom I am well pleased" (Mark 1:11). This statement seems to be a fulfilment of the prophecy in Isaiah 42:1, as well as perhaps of Psalm 2:7. Following the temptation to which Mark refers only briefly (Mark 1:13), Jesus proceeded to Galilee preaching the good news of the gospel of the kingdom of God and saying the kingdom was at hand. He called upon men to repent and believe the gospel. In this message he also set forth one of the basic essentials of the missionary message of the ages: that he himself is the King, the promised Son of David, the long-awaited Messiah. In his coming, the kingdom was at hand. That kingdom had world dimensions. Every man, everywhere, without regard to circumstance, might through repentance and belief in Christ claim the gracious privilege of entrance to this kingdom. His kingdom was to be one of righteousness, peace, and truth. The gospel he proclaimed was truly good news!

The Jews who had failed to see the purpose of God in the ages had continued too long for a restoration of the earthly kingdom of David. They had anticipated a ruler like David who would sit on an earthly throne. A far higher kingdom, however, was at hand and a far greater King. Of this King, David was only a type. From the brief review above, it is obvious then that even in the early message Jesus is said to have proclaimed in Galilee, there is set forth at least a suggestion of the purpose of his coming. That purpose contained the glorious missionary objective of establishing his reign universally in the hearts of men.

The Purpose Proclaimed in Matthew

Matthew began his Gospel by tracing the ancestry of Jesus back to Abraham. His purpose was apparently to reveal that Jesus Christ is the true Messiah, the Anointed One, and the promised descendant of David and of Abraham. The genealogy itself thus has genuine missionary implications. It intentionally unfolds the fulfilment of God's ancient promise to Israel. (Luke's genealogy, though it traces the lineage of Jesus all the way back to God, has a similar purpose, but also stresses the deity, as well as the humanity of Jesus.)

It was to Abraham that the covenant had first been given. Matthew called attention to this, declaring that the covenant made with Abraham was in truth fulfilled in Christ; and the great prophetic hope of the Messiah had its realization also in him.

Matthew's purpose becomes clearer as we examine the angelic revelation given to Joseph: "Thou shalt call his name Jesus: for he shall save his people from their sins" (Matt. 1:21). (The name "Jesus" means Saviour.) The explanation which follows in the text indicates the reason why Jesus was thus named. Matthew added: "Now all this was done, that it might be fulfilled which was spoken of the Lord by the prophet, saying, Behold, a virgin shall be with child, and shall bring forth a son, and they shall call his name Emmanuel, which being interpreted is, God with us" (Matt. 1:22-23). Matthew's reference is clearly to Isaiah 7:14.

In the coming of Christ, God was taking the necessary step to span the gulf between himself, the infinite Spirit, and man. Later John explained that the "Word was made flesh, and dwelt among us" (John 1:14). Man in his limited nature could not become God or rise to God; but God, the Creator, could "come" to man and even dwell with him. This, however, necessitated the Incarnation. That Incarnation, of course, would have a significance reaching beyond all human barriers, whether of race, tongue, or nation.

Matthew proceeded to reveal that Jesus is "King of the Jews." He possibly had in mind Jeremiah 23:5, which reads, "Behold, the days come, saith the Lord, that I will raise unto David a righteous Branch, and a King shall reign and prosper, and shall execute judgment and justice in the earth." Zechariah also had said: "Rejoice greatly, O daughter of Zion; shout, O daughter of Jerusalem: behold, thy King cometh unto thee" (Zech. 9:9). Matthew may, moreover, have had in mind Numbers 24:17: "I shall see him, but not now: I shall behold him, but not nigh: there shall come a Star out of Jacob, and a Sceptre shall rise out of Israel, and shall smite the corners of Moab, and destroy all the children of Sheth." It is clear from Matthew, however, that the One promised above was to be no mere Jewish sovereign. He would belong to all nations. As evidence of this, Matthew introduced in this very context the account of the coming of the Magi, the wise men from the East. These were distinguished representatives of other nations. They, too, came to offer their allegiance and to worship Jesus. This event itself had missionary overtones. Christ, of course, was destined to be King of kings and Lord of lords. To him at last, not only representatives of other nations, but every knee will bow and every tongue will confess. He alone has power to save. In his rule alone can men everywhere find peace and hope, a mighty motive for missions.

The Purpose Proclaimed in Luke

Of all the Gospels, Luke gives the fullest account of the birth of Christ. It begins with Luke's record of what the angel said to Zacharias. Zacharias was told that his wife was to bear a son whom they should call John. "And he shall go before him [Jesus] in the spirit and power of Elias, to turn the hearts of the fathers to the children, and the disobedient to the wisdom of the just; to make ready a people prepared for the Lord" (Luke 1:17). This is a reference to Malachi 4:5-6 and Isaiah 40:3. The *Amplified New Testament* helps us to see the statement of purpose contained here. It reads: "And he will [himself] go before him in the spirit and power of Elijah, to turn back the hearts of the fathers to the children, and the disobedient and incredulous and unpersuadable to the wisdom of the upright [which is the knowledge and holy love of the will of God], in order to make ready for the Lord a people [perfectly] prepared—in spirit, adjusted and disposed and placed in the right moral state." John's work as forerunner of Jesus was to lead men to true repentance and thus to preparedness for the coming of the Lord.

1:17

Luke reported that the angel became more explicit to Mary, who was engaged to be married to Joseph: "And the angel said unto her, Fear not, Mary: for thou hast found favour with God. And, behold, thou shalt conceive in thy womb, and bring forth a son, and shalt call his name JESUS. He shall be great, and shall be called the Son of the Highest: and the Lord God shall give unto him the throne of his father David: and he shall reign over the house of Jacob for ever; and of his kingdom there shall be no end" (Luke 1:30-33). Luke wanted us to know that the Son born of the virgin Mary fulfilled the predictions made in Isaiah 9:6-7. He was called "the Son of the Most High" and is to occupy the throne of David forever. Obviously, no mere earthly throne was in mind, as it is to be occupied "forever." Nor does the reference to the house of Judah in this context appear to change this fact.

Mary was later moved to predict that all generations, for all ages to come, would call her blessed. The birth of Jesus, she saw, would give expression to the universal mercy of God. It would reveal his compassion toward the afflicted from generation to generation and age to age (Luke 1:50). Justice would be wielded by this one to come; powers and thrones would be subject to his will (Luke 1:51-52). All of this, she recognized, was to be the fulfilment of the promise made to Abraham (Luke 1:55).

Mary's song (Luke 1:46-55) is a poetic expression with deep missionary meaning. Mary was inspired to see that in the coming of this Son, God's mercy would be visited upon all men, and his justice would at last prevail in the earth. Though she had her own people primarily in mind, it is clear that all men somehow were affected.

Later Zacharias, the father of John, saw that in the events to take place God was bringing deliverance and redemption to his people. He was sure the promises of the prophets were being fulfilled in the birth of John and in the coming of the one whom John would announce. He also saw justice to be a consequence of what God was doing and that the compassion of God was being expressed through it all. He was confident, moreover, that the covenant which God sealed by "the oath which he sware to our father Abraham" (Luke 1:73) was now being realized. To him it was clear that John, his son, would go before to make ready the way and to bring the knowledge of salvation to those who were longing for remission of their sins.

Luke added that Zacharias was inspired to say the "dayspring from on high hath visited us, to give light to them that sit in darkness and in the shadow of death, to guide our feet into the way of peace" (Luke 1:78-79). This marvelous display of God's gracious mercies was in reality a dawning of hope on earth. Since the birth of Christ it has never been, nor can it ever be, utterly dark again.

The announcement to the shepherds on the Judean hills, "For unto you is born this day in the city of David a Saviour, which is Christ the Lord" (Luke 2:11), set a note ringing down the ages, as did the song of the angelic host: "Glory to God in the highest, and on earth peace, good will toward men" (Luke 2:14). The assurance here given has become the hope and inspiration of all nations to which it is known. It was, indeed, good news. Micah had prophesied: "But thou, Bethlehem Ephratah, though thou be little among the thousands of Judah, yet out of thee shall he come forth unto me that is to be ruler in Israel; whose goings forth have been from of old, from everlasting" (Micah 5:2).

Eight days after his birth Jesus was taken to the Temple for his "purification." There an aged disciple Simeon, moved by the Holy Spirit, spoke also of the fulfilment of God's promise of salvation: "For mine eyes have seen thy salvation, which thou hast prepared before the face of all people; a light to lighten the Gentiles, and the glory of thy people Israel" (Luke 2:30-32).

2:30-32

How significant this moving declaration is. It points, not only to the fulfilment of the hope of a Messiah for the Jew, but also to one who should bring salvation to the Gentiles as well. Simeon forewarned Mary that, not only was Christ to be appointed for the fall and rising of many in Israel, but also that "a sword" would pierce through her own soul. This seems clearly a foreshadowing of the cross upon which Christ died for the whole world.

The Purpose Proclaimed in John

Although John was likely the last Gospel written, the prologue of the book points farther back than does any one of the other accounts in the Gospels. Luke admittedly traced Jesus' genealogy (Luke 3:23-38) back through Abraham to God; but he did not interpret, as did John, the significance of what he had in mind. John set down a record of events and discourses associated with Christ in the days of his flesh. He also gave us the theological and mystical meaning of it all.

John, as one of the twelve, had enjoyed two or three years of close association with Jesus. With great certainty John portrayed Jesus as God himself, as eternally "one" with the Father as well as with the Holy Spirit, as the source of all creation, and as the light and the life of men. John was writing not merely for his own people, the Jews, but for all men. Christ, he declared, is the true (real) light, the light which "lighteth every man that cometh into the world." No man can know God except through Jesus. Jesus reveals the true likeness of the Father and makes known also what God expects of men and how men may come to God. John the Baptist was sent to bear witness, the apostle says, of that light. The purpose of his witness was "that all men through him might believe" (John 1:7).

The more one looks at the first accounts of Christ's coming into the world, the more overwhelming becomes the evidence that missions lay at the very center of it all. It was the true essence of his glorious advent. Those who set down the Gospel records of his coming somehow were made to see beyond their own vision. They saw the universal purpose God had in mind in this event. They saw that God's compassion is to be revealed to *all* men. His justice is to affect *all* men. His salvation is for *all* men. Christ is the Light of *all* men.

Every forlorn soul sitting in darkness anywhere in the world and learning the good news of Christ's coming may rejoice, knowing that the angelic announcement, "For unto you is born . . . a Saviour," is for him, too. All who find him as Saviour, moreover, are privileged—and appointed—to bear witness of that light which, according to John, is as the sunrise to all who sit in darkness everywhere.

2—Missions in the Message of Regeneration

Matthew 3:1 to 4:12; Mark 1:2-14; Luke 3:3 to 4:14; John 1:19 to 4:45

The literary masters of our day, with but few exceptions, seem to sound the one common note of "gloom and doom." Many have apparently embraced a cold naturalism, totally without belief in God.

It is doubtful that pessimism was ever as deep as now. And for what reason? Could the reason be man's refusal to make a proper response to God? to accept God's work of regeneration? While every man has turned to his own way, depending upon science and learning to save him, the needs of the soul have been forgotten. Hence, in the hour of man's greatest achievements in the natural realm, the world may be suffering its greatest need in the spiritual realm. In such a time, how deep is the need to restudy God's plan of redemption and regeneration and its purpose!

In the opening verses of the Fourth Gospel we read of Christ: "He came unto his own, and his own received him not. But as many as received him, to them he gave the power to become the sons of God, even to them that believe on his name: which were born not of blood, nor of the will of the flesh, nor of the will of man, but of God" (John 1:11-13). Here is revealed the secret of how man can be changed, of how he can become truly a child of God. And nothing is more important.

The present study is an examination of the early portion of each of the Gospels, especially as these sections reveal Christ's work of regeneration. Christ came to be the Saviour of man. John the Baptist, the promised forerunner, soon came preaching in the wilderness of Judea, saying: "Repent ye: for the kingdom of heaven is at hand" (Matt. 3:2).

Repentance is literally a change of mind, motivated by regret, and accompanied by a change of conduct. John insisted that those who professed repentance should give proof by bringing forth "fruits worthy of repentance" (Luke 3:8). This would require a changed relationship to others and a changed attitude toward God. Men were not to depend on anything else to save them, but were rather to look only to God by faith.

True repentance meant that relationships with others were to be straightened out; justice was to be done; wrong and injustice were to cease. "He that hath two coats, let him impart to him that hath none; and he that hath meat, let him do likewise" (Luke 3:11). Sin is first an offense against God. Repentance, therefore, must first be "toward God." But it cannot stop there. Unless one is right with his fellowman, he cannot be fully right with God. Repentance is followed by regeneration, which is followed by reconciliation.

John urged men to repent because, "The kingdom of heaven [was] at hand" (Matt. 3:2).

John preached that Jesus would baptize men "with the Holy Ghost, and with fire" (Matt. 3:11), and introduced Christ as "The Lamb of God, which taketh away the sin of the world" (John 1:29). "He that believeth on the Son hath everlasting life," he further declared, "He that believeth not the Son shall not see life; but the wrath of God abideth on him" (John 3:36).

True repentance leads to the possession through Christ of eternal life. It is real and true life now; and, as Jesus would later say, "life more abundantly" (John 10:10).

It now seems appropriate to turn to some of the encounters of Jesus, as found in the early pages of the Gospels, and to see from them what resulted. First, Jesus himself was met by the tempter (Matt. 4:1-11). From this encounter, several facts about the needs of men and the purposes of Christ are suggested. An example is seen in Jesus' declaration that "Man shall not live by bread alone" (Matt. 4:4). One of the greatest temptations man has ever faced is the temptation to believe his major concern should be his own physical needs. To be sure, physical needs are important, but man cannot live only by satisfying them.

The tempter also tried to get Jesus to fall down and worship him, promising that in this way Jesus could surely have the world as his own. Satan boldly claimed, "That [the world] is delivered unto me" (Luke 4:6). How had the world been "delivered" to the tempter? Man's decision to disobey his Maker and disbelieve the God who gave him life, his false worship of himself, his forgetfulness of his own spiritual nature and need had "delivered" the world over to the tempter! But Christ would not have the world back on the terms of the tempter. Man in his rebellion toward God may rejoice in the encouragement the radical and misguided give him by declaring, "God is dead." Yet it is ever true that the only way one can reach his highest fulfilment is to heed the declaration: "Thou shalt worship the Lord thy God, and him only shalt thou serve" (Luke 4:8). The supreme folly of man is to believe that if he will only bow down to the devil and serve him, he can find real life and hope.

Let us now examine some of the encounters of Christ with people, and their responses to him. After John the Baptist had made his introduction of Jesus as the "Lamb of God, which taketh away the sins of the world," Andrew and Simon Peter, his brother, sought to know Jesus more intimately (John 1:35-42). Andrew had become convinced Jesus was the Messiah and later brought his brother Simon to him. Both Andrew and Simon trusted in Jesus and evidently found in him all they had ever desired to meet their spiritual needs. Jesus, looking upon Simon and knowing the change that would take place in his life by his coming to Jesus, gave Simon a new name. The name has identified him ever since: "Thou shalt be called Cephas, which is by interpretation, a stone" (John 1:42). A moody Simon was now to become, through the regenerating power of Christ, solid like a rock in character and in steadfastness. Although apparently no change of name was given to Andrew, it is evident that he, too, found soul-satisfaction in Jesus. Wherever he appeared in the Gospel accounts, he was always bringing someone to Jesus, as the lad with the little lunch, which was to be multiplied to feed the five thousand and the Greeks who later sought to "see" Jesus. Andrew seemed confident that what men needed they could find in Jesus.

The Gospel of John next tells of the conversion of Philip and Nathanael (John 1:43-51). Jesus on meeting Philip had said "Follow me." So great was the experience of Philip, that he soon sought his friend, Nathanael, and invited him to come and see for himself what Jesus could do for him.

The well-known interview with Jesus sought by Nicodemus, the

Pharisee (John 3:1-18), is one of the most revealing in the Gospels as to how Jesus changes men. This wealthy, well-trained, and intelligent member of the Sanhedrin was likely one of the noblest and best men of his day. He had been zealous to keep all the law and to do everything which he thought God required. Yet there was a void within, an aching vacuum which cried out to be filled. Not all of his personal goodness and self-righteousness satisfied his sense of spiritual need. Hence, he was drawn to Jesus for a personal discussion of his need. Jesus, well understanding the spiritual hunger of Nicodemus, declared: "Verily, verily, I say unto thee except a man be born again, he cannot see the kingdom of God" (John 3:3). Even the best and the most devout like Nicodemus must experience this change, or they will never "see" the kingdom. Nothing else can substitute. However much the religions or philosophies of the world may help, nothing short of the changing by the Holy Spirit into newness of life through Christ Jesus can save men. This is one of the basic reasons why the work of missions can never end, until the last man in the world has had opportunity to know how he may become a new creation in Christ Jesus.

Contrasted with the pious Nicodemus is the woman of Sychar, who met Jesus at Jacob's well (John 4:5-42). All that Nicodemus was in character and conduct, this woman was not. She was evidently conscious of a thirst for something better. This woman was led by Jesus to a confession of her own need and to a discovery that in him she could find "a well of water springing up into everlasting life" (John 4:14). Though the figure of speech Jesus used in talking with this woman was different from the one used with Nicodemus, it meant the same thing. This woman could be changed from within and this would change her life. She joyously accepted what Christ offered her. Forgetting her waterpots, the woman ran back to the city to declare to all she met: "Come, see a man, which told me all things that ever I did: is not this the Christ?" (John 4:29). In consequence of her testimony, many from the city went out also to see Christ. Many, too, testified later. "Now we believe, not because of thy saying: for we have heard him ourselves, and know that this is indeed the Christ, the Saviour of the world" (John 4:42).

No matter how deep is the moral need of men and women in our day Christ, if truly accepted, is adequate to meet it. Here is another compelling motive for missionary endeavor.

3—Missions in the Mission of the Disciples

Matthew 6:17 to 8:33; Mark 1:14 to 3:21; Luke 4:14 to 10:24; John 1:35 to 4:46

"The missionary enterprise," says Robert Hall Glover, "is no human conception or understanding, or invention, no mere philanthropy. . . . It did not originate in the brain of man, not even of William Carey, or the apostle Paul. Its source was in the heart of God. And Jesus Christ, God's missionary to a lost world, was the supreme revelation of his heart and expression of his love."

Just so! Indeed, is not this what the recurrent Christmas story reaffirms and what the gospel is really all about (John 3:16; 2 Cor. 9:15)? "For unto us a child is born, unto us a son is given" (Isa. 9:6).

Jesus is thus truly the "one sent"—the first great missionary—God's gift of love to save the world. *But the great issue of all time is man's response to this gift.* In this chapter we shall observe some of the early responses of men to that gift.

We saw in the previous chapter what happened to Nicodemus, to a woman of Sychar, and to others when they believed on Jesus. We saw how the woman who had obtained "living water" from Jesus at Jacob's well ran back with that story to her village and told it with such moving appeal that many in the town believed. Those who truly believed on Jesus thereafter shared their faith. And this was what the Lord expected. The supreme mission of the disciples became, not merely their privilege of knowing Jesus, but their joyous, though often costly, task of "catching men." To this work they were called, and to this ministry they were assigned.

There seems to be clear evidence in the Gospels that missions really began much earlier than the return of the disciples from the Mount of Ascension. Indeed, the disciples at first became missionaries voluntarily and without formal appointment. Later, however, Jesus began to send them out by special commission. The history of missions is the history of this "sending."

All Followers Are Missionaries

All followers of Christ are missionaries, but specific assignments are given to many. They thus become missionaries with definite appointment.

The Gospels of Matthew, Mark, and Luke all tell significantly of the first call of Christ to his followers for specific service (Luke 5:1-11; Mark 1:16-20; Matt. 4:18-22). By the shores of Galilee, Jesus found Simon and Andrew, James and John, and called these four fishermen to become fishers of men. "Fear not," he said to Peter, "from henceforth thou shalt catch men" (Luke 5:10). All four of these men were henceforth engaged in this work. Two, if not all of them, had already met Jesus and believed on him (John 1:35-42). Now they were called specifically to be "disciples" and were assigned a mission. That mission was to "catch men." Later Jesus called Matthew (Mark 2:13-17; Matt. 9:9-13; Luke 5:27-32); and still later, he selected twelve of his followers to be apostles. These included the four brothers, Andrew and Peter, James and John, as well as Matthew (Mark 3:13-19; Luke 6:12-16). What a variety of personality and background is seen in these men! Andrew was evidently a quiet, retiring personality, yet with deep commitment. Peter, on the other hand, was outgoing, impulsive, and quick to speak. James and John were called "sons of thunder," implying that each was quick tempered and explosive. Yet we know that John was also a man of tender and deep emotions, who seemed more able than any other New Testament writer to understand the depths of God's love. Nathaniel was apparently a highly practical man who demanded evidence before he believed, yet he possessed deep understanding. Thomas, often called the doubter, always demanded convincing evidence before he would commit himself. Matthew (Levi) evidently had business sense and believed in looking after only his own interests. Though a Jew, he had obtained the right to be a tax collector for the hated Romans. Among the twelve was also the shrewd, selfish, and grasping Judas Iscariot, later called a thief. He seems not to have been a believer but was called as the devil's witness, who would finally be forced to admit he had betrayed "innocent blood."

The Call and Assignment of the Twelve

The special call and assignment given the twelve make it obvious that any type personality and background can be instrumental in carrying out the divine missionary purpose. Mark, indeed, says of Jesus that he called "whom he would" (Mark 3:13).

Mark specified also the purpose of the call given the disciples: "to preach, and to have power to heal sicknesses, and to cast out devils" (Mark 3:14-15). This work was evidently to be a part of the disciples' task in "catching men." But what were the disciples to preach, and how were they to "cast out devils"? The answer likely is seen in what Jesus himself was preaching and how he was meeting the needs of men: "And Jesus went about all Galilee, teaching in their synagogues, and preaching the gospel of the kingdom, and healing all manner of sickness and all manner of disease among the people. And his fame went throughout all Syria: and they brought unto him all sick people that were taken with divers diseases and torments, and those which were possessed with devils, and those which were lunatick, and those that had the palsy; and he healed them" (Matt. 4:23-24). If the disciples were to do what their Master was doing, they were first to preach the gospel of the kingdom. As seen in a previous chapter, this was the "good news" of the reign of Christ in the hearts of men and of the presence of his kingdom. This was distinctly a missionary message.

In the work of the Master, however, there was not only the ministry of preaching and delivering from devils but also of healing. Jesus looked upon the multitudes with compassion and was sensitive to their physical needs. He healed the demoniac (Mark 1:23-28); Peter's mother-in-law (Mark 1:29-34); the leper (Mark 1:40-45; Matt. 8:2-4; Luke 5:12-16); the paralytic let down through the roof (Mark 2:1-12; Matt. 9:1-8; Luke 5:17-25); the lame man at the pool (John 5:1-13); and many others.

We are told significantly: "The people sought him, and came unto him, and stayed him, that he should not depart from them. And he said unto them, I must preach the kingdom of God to other cities also: for therefore am I sent" (Luke 4:42-43). Mark quoted Jesus as saying: "Let us go into the next towns, that I may preach there also: for therefore came I forth" (Mark 1:38). Great as was his concern for any one area, and great as was the need found there, he must take the good news elsewhere also. This, we may judge, was one reason why Jesus soon decided to send the twelve on a special mission. Thus he would extend the reach of what he was doing. Seeing the multitudes "scattered abroad, as sheep having no shepherd," he said to the disciples: "The harvest truly is plenteous, but the labourers are few" (Matt. 9:37). His compassion was the prelude to his decision to send out the twelve. That same compassion, we must believe, continues to be his reason for sending laborers into the harvest.

Specific Assignments Made to His Followers

Jesus' specific assignments of missionary service to his disciples came, according to the Gospel accounts, in at least three different stages. They were (1) the sending out of twelve, (2) the sending forth of the seventy, (3) the Great Commission given after the resurrection.

The mission of the twelve and of the seventy apparently had much in common *(compare Matt. 10:1-33 with Luke 10:1-24).* Jesus gave to the twelve authority over unclean spirits, to cast them out, and the power to heal diseases and sicknesses of various kinds. Luke especially noted that Jesus sent the twelve forth "to preach the kingdom of God, and to heal the sick" (Luke 9:2). The twelve, like the seventy, were to go by two's, and were not to go either to the Gentiles or the Samaritans, but to the "lost sheep of the house Israel" (Matt. 10:6). They went to preach, saying "the kingdom of heaven is at hand," and to heal the sick, raise the dead, cleanse the lepers, and cast out devils. In other words, their ministry was to be like that of their Master. They were apparently to go from city to city and even from village to village as he was doing throughout the Galilean region. Theirs was to be a home missions task of evangelism and of ministry to the needs of men.

Jesus' restricted commission to the twelve, confining their labors to the Jews, must not be misunderstood. Later he was to expand this commission to include the whole world, but now a place of beginning was necessary. The Jews, through whom God had worked so long to effect his purpose in behalf of the world, were the logical people to whom the message should first come. Although it appears the twelve were assigned to towns and villages of Galilee, apparently the seventy took in a wider latitude, possibly including Judah and Perea.

Witness to All Mankind

The seventy were commanded to say: "The kingdom of God is come nigh unto you" (Luke 10:9-11). So successful was the work of the seventy that they returned to Jesus with joy saying: "Lord, even the devils are subject unto us through thy name" (Luke 10:17). God never calls one to do what he will not enable him to do.

Although there is divided opinion upon the matter, it seems the seventy did not include the apostles in their number. This fact accounts in part for their amazement at their success, and also points to the truth that others besides those especially called to the ministry can be fruitful missionaries. Although Jesus informed the seventy that they were not so much to rejoice that the "spirits" had been subject unto them but that their names were written in heaven, he is said to have rejoiced in the Holy Spirit himself following the reports of the seventy (Luke 10:21).

Throughout the account concerning the seventy, there were overtones of the universal concern of the Master. Soon those overtones became explicit. In truth, in the same chapter in which the record of the sending out of the seventy is given, Luke gave Jesus' story of the good Samaritan. The point of this story was to show how a Samaritan was fulfilling God's standard of loving his neighbor as himself, even though that neighbor was a Jew and thus a member of a despised race. Jesus repeatedly sought to lift the sights of the disciples to behold the whole world. He had said, *"God so loved the world,"* "the field is the *world,"* "I am the light of the *world,"* "I, if I be lifted up from the earth, will draw *all men* unto me," and *"other sheep* I have, which are not of this fold: *them also* I must bring." Finally, he was to expand the commission given the disciples to include *all nations.* The commission is thus universal: "Go . . . and teach *all* nations," preach the gospel to *every* creature, and "ye shall be witnesses . . . unto the *uttermost part* of the earth," he ordered. Those to whom the Great Commission first came included the disciples, the seventy, the "hundred and twenty" of Acts 1, and possibly the above "five hundred," who, Paul said (1 Cor. 15:6), saw the risen Lord. From the beginning, it seems clear then that those who embrace Christ as Lord are expected to become missionaries. The responses of individuals, the assignments given the twelve and the seventy, and the Great Commission following the resurrection all point to the conclusion that the mission of the followers of Christ is missions.

4—Missions and the Ministry of Healing

Matthew 8:14 to 20:34

"He was wounded for our transgressions . . . and with his stripes we are healed" (Isa. 53:5).

"And there came a leper . . . And Jesus, moved with compassion, put forth his hand, and touched him, and saith unto him . . . be thou clean" (Mark 1:40-41).

Christians believe they can respond in more than one way to the Great Commission. One of these is through medical missions.

Christ's Healing Ministry

But what do hospitals, doctors, and nurses have to do with missions? Can their efforts really be justified from the Bible? A study of the healing ministry of Christ answers such questions at once and finally. One cannot read the Gospels without seeing what a large place Jesus gave to the ministry of healing. He repeatedly stated this work as a part of the task of his disciples. More than twenty specific instances of Jesus' own healing are also set down in the four Gospels. Among those healed were:

a nobleman's son (John 4:46-54)
Peter's mother-in-law (Mark 1:29-34; Matt. 8:14-17; Luke 4:38-41)
a leper (Mark 1:40-45; Matt. 8:2-4; Luke 5:12-16)
a paralytic (Mark 2:1-12; Matt. 9:1-8; Luke 5:17-26)
a lame man at the pool (John 5:1-15)

a man with a withered hand (Mark 3:1-6; Matt. 12:9-14; Luke 6:6-11)
a considerable group (Mark 3:7-12; Matt. 12:15-21)
a centurion's servant (Matt. 8:5-13; Luke 7:1-10)
a widow's son raised from the dead (Luke 7:11-17)
a Gadarene demoniac (Mark 5:1-20; Matt. 8:28-34; Luke 8:26-39)
Jairus' daughter and a woman with an issue of blood (Mark 5:21-34; Matt. 9:18-26; Luke 8:40-56)
two blind men (Matt. 9:27-34)
a Syrophenician's daughter (Mark 7:24-30; Matt. 15:21-28)
a man deaf and dumb (Mark 7:31-37; Matt. 15:29-31)
a blind man of Bethsaida (Mark 8:22-26)
a demoniac boy (Mark 9:14-29; Matt. 17:14-20; Luke 9:37-43)
a man born blind (John 9)
a crippled woman (Luke 13:10-17)
Lazarus raised from the dead (John 11)
blind Bartimaeus (Mark 10:46-52; Matt. 20:29-34; Luke 18:35-43).

One of the first instances of healing by Christ apparently was that of the nobleman's son. This nobleman is said to have come to Cana to ask Jesus to heal his child. This man was a royal official and possibly a member of the household of Herod. It is striking that a courtier such as he should have come to a carpenter. What a remarkable work that carpenter must already have done to draw such men as this to him! Of particular note is the fact that this needy man must have been considered totally unworthy by the Jews. Jesus was moved with compassion by his request and expression of faith, and he healed the boy.

In the touching account of the healing of the leper (Mark 1:40-45) who came to Jesus pleading, "If thou wilt, thou canst make me clean" (v. 40), it is said again that Jesus was moved with compassion and stretched out his hand and touched the leper (who else would have then touched a leper?) saying (literally), I *desire* it. Be cleansed at once. How revealing this answer is! Jesus also desires the healing, the wholeness, of every man.

In connection with the healing of Peter's mother-in-law, Matthew noted he healed all that came that evening. This ministry, Matthew added, was in fulfilment of the prophecy of Isaiah (53:4-5), "Himself took our infirmities, and bare our sicknesses" (Matt. 8:17). Jesus' work of healing, judging from these instances and others which could be cited, was not merely a means to a spiritual end.

It is said in most instances that he healed men because of his own compassion. Medical missions, we conclude, is a further expression of that same compassion.

Man's Greater Spiritual Need

Jesus made clear, however, in more than one instance that the spiritual need of a man is more serious than his physical need. The case of his healing the man borne by four appears to teach as much (Mark 2:1-12). He first forgave this man's sin before he healed him, thereby placing the man's spiritual need before his physical need.

Jesus' primary mission was to make men entirely whole. No one can be truly "well" unless he is cured from within, unless he can experience regeneration and renewing of his spiritual life. Yet, because Jesus was interested in the whole man, and because he knew so well the interrelationship between one's spiritual and physical health, he was always concerned also to relieve physical needs. His healing work, moreover, had an impressive impact on others beside those healed. Following the healing of the paralytic it is said: "They were all amazed, and glorified God" (Mark 2:12). Possibly many of the multitude who afterward followed Jesus were persuaded to put their trust in him because of what they saw him do for others.

In a comparative study of the healing of the lame man at the pool (John 5:1-15) and of the man born blind (John 9), it is interesting to note that the former's condition was likely a consequence of sin. In the latter, however, no guilt of either the blind man or his parents was involved. Although Jesus recognized sin as the cause of some illness, this did not keep him from exercising compassion toward them and healing them. Jesus' remarks in connection with the man born blind suggest that some, if not all, physical affliction gives occasion for the "works of God [to be] made manifest" (John 9:3). Divine compassion and power can be disclosed to ones with physical afflictions, and thus men can be led to see what God is like. This truth has a powerful meaning for medical missions. The depth and vastness of suffering today defy comprehension. But in the ministry of Christians to those who suffer, God, we believe, is glorified and his power to save manifested. This fact alone makes medical missions most needful.

Of course true Christian compassion demands a response to

suffering. To be like Christ who was among men as one that serves, we must serve. Next to helping men to find freedom from guilt and newness of life in Christ stands service which brings wholeness to the body and relief from pain. They who love as Christ loved cannot ignore the cry of physical need. This is a lesson of abiding significance.

Partners in Medical Missions

Another lesson disclosed in the Gospel accounts of healing is that others besides the afflicted often have a vital, decisive part in what happens. The account of the paralytic is an example. The four who brought the paralytic to Jesus were remarkable both for their determination and their faith. They could not be discouraged or turned away. They found a way to get the man into the presence of Christ. The Scriptures pointedly remark that "When Jesus saw their faith, he said unto the sick of the palsy, Son, thy sins be forgiven thee" (Mark 2:5). Persistence and faith brought results. Through support of medical missions every Christian has opportunity to be among "the four." If our determination is deep enough and our faith great enough, we can increasingly participate in this glorious work.

No Bounds to Christ's Concern

A further lesson from accounts of Jesus' healing is that there was apparently no kind of physical need which did not know his concern. He did not refuse even those whose condition had been caused by their own sins. Fever, leprosy, paralysis, lameness, a withered hand, blindness, deafness, an impediment of speech, an issue of blood, and even diseases of the mind concerned him. He responded to the tortured mental condition of the Gadarene demoniac and to the plight of the epileptic boy (Matt. 17:15). He even reached into the casket of the widow's son and into the tomb of Lazarus to call back to life some who were dead. The whole scale of human need won his compassion, whether that need was physical, mental, or spiritual.

Reference has been made to the faith of the four who brought the paralytic to Jesus. In a number of instances such as that of the Syrophenician woman, the centurion, and Jairus, Jesus responded solely to the faith of others than those who were ill. In other cases, like that of the leper or the two blind men, it was the faith of the afflicted themselves which moved him.

Faith is always an important element in healing, whether it be faith in the doctor, the nurses, medical science, or what. But faith firmly placed in Christ is of immeasurable worth. Many outstanding Christian medical men believe, with others of us, that in the final analysis all healing is from God. This does not mean, however, that the knowledge and power given to medical science are needless. They, too, are gifts of God.

God Responds to Man's Concern

A further truth which seems evident from a study of the healing ministry of Christ is that the depth of *concern* of those trying to do the work of healing had a bearing on results. This is especially suggested by the case of the demoniac boy (Mark 9:14-29). When the perplexed disciples asked Jesus why they could not "cast him out," he replied, according to Mark, "This kind can come forth by nothing, but by prayer and fasting" (Mark 9:29). Matthew added, "Because of your unbelief" (Matt. 17:20). Could it have been Christ was saying to his disciples, not only that they had really not prayed with faith, but also that their concern for this lad was not deep enough to make their prayer meaningful?

Another truth seems evident from a careful analysis of the healing work of Christ. It is that his ministry was impartial. It did not regard one's social estate, financial circumstances, race, or nation. He responded to the petition of the Roman centurion and to the entreaty of the Syrophenician woman, both Gentiles. His compassion knew no barriers.

A Witness to Man's Concern

"Medical missions," says Edwin E. White, has been "a most effective means, though not at all the only means, demonstrating the Christian conviction of the priceless value of every man, woman, and child in the sight of God. Christianity's care for every man has been effectively set forth in missionary endeavors, especially to unfortunate groups, whose condition in many lands has been pitiable." Dr. White further states: "Men and women have had to catch something of Christ's spirit before they could thus devote themselves to the profession of healing, not for gain, but that they might minister to those in need."

In the light of the healing ministry of Christ the opinion expressed by a missionary leader deserves again to be heard: "A distinction between the different functions and ministries [of Christians] can never be made by acclaiming different values and priorities. One often hears that gospel proclamation has priority. That is true only if proclamation refers to word and deed, as well as to all gifts given to the individual . . . [By] medical missions, we can show to others the compassionate love which has been shown to us. In a world in which the word of man is questioned, we can say and prove that we know the love of God which seeks every man. Where race and caste divide people, we may bear witness to our faith that every man has worth before God."

"Health is involved in life," says Charles H. Germany, "and the meaning and purpose of life are central to the mission of the church. We are being led biblically, theologically, and by life's experiences to the issue of the healing ministry in the mission of the church."

Ought we not to capture anew the spirit revealed in 3 John: "Beloved, I wish above all things that thou mayest prosper and be in *health,* even as thy soul prospereth" (v. 2).

Evangelism, meaning only the proclamation of the gospel and the winning of souls to Christ, is by some considered the only legitimate form of the missionary task. Others have tended to hold that service alone—medical, educational, relief—fulfils the Great Commission. Creighton Lacy well says, "All Christians must hold these two tasks in one inseparable purpose."

5—Missions and the Message of the Parables

Matthew 13:1-58; 20:1-16; 22:1-14; 25:1-46

No one reading the Gospels could avoid the parables of our Lord—and no one would want to. It has been well said that "the parables are the characteristic messages of Jesus . . . his most persuasive. . . . A prosier teaching might not break our stubborn will, but the sight of the father running to welcome his wayward son leaves us 'defenseless utterly' " (Buttrick).

The parables of Jesus truly possess the secret of eternal truth. They are not simply stories. "They are instruments of a transcendent purpose. When we turn to them only as illustrations of everyday morality, or commonplace homiletical discourse, we miss a great deal of the significance of Jesus for his time and for all times—including our own" (Smith). Examination of the parables will reveal that they, not only speak directly to our times, but also assure us concerning Jesus' love for the whole world in his purpose and mission. This chapter examines some of the parables to see what they do say regarding the great missionary enterprise. As the parables relate to various aspects of the Master's teaching, not all of them could be called specifically missionary in character. Yet even some of these, like the parables which illustrate the conflict between the old order and the new have some relationship to missions. Examples are the new patch on the old garment (Luke 5:36; Matt. 9:16; Mark 2:21); new wine in old wine skins (Luke 5:37-39; Matt. 9:17; Mark 2:22); and the new treasures and the old (Matt. 13:51-52). They point up the tension inevitably created by the proclamation of the gospel and the demands of the kingdom.

In a similar way some of the parables referring to the kingdom may be understood as having at least indirect significance for missions. Dr. J. B. Lawrence has well said: "Jesus spoke in world terms. He took the Old Testament conception of the kingdom and gave it a vastly richer meaning than Jewish traditional teaching has ever given. He transformed the kingdom from a national ideal to a goal of universal significance (Luke 4:43; Matt. 24:14). He did not think of the kingdom of God as having geographical, or racial, or political, or social, or cultural boundary lines (Matt. 12:50). He saw men coming from all quarters of the globe and entering into it (Luke 13:29). 'Whosoever will' is the boundary line he gave to the kingdom."

A Priceless Possession

Several parables, such as the hidden treasures (Matt. 13:44) and the pearl of great price (Matt. 13:45-46), reveal the superior worth of the kingdom, surpassing every other possession. This truth is at the heart of the missionary message.

There are other parables such as that of the growing seed (Mark 4:26-29), the mustard seed (Mark 4:30-32), and the leaven (Matt. 13:33), which reveal the method of the growth and the spreading influence of the kingdom. On the assurances of Christian growth these parables provide, the missionary enterprise gains hope of success in its labors. Evidence that this hope is valid exists in terms of professions of faith in Christ and growth of Christian groups. Evidence also exists in the fact that even certain non-Christian religions are now attempting to imitate Christians in some of their practices.

The way of entrance into the kingdom and of reconciliation with God is also shown in certain parables. Such is especially true of the parable of the prodigal son (Luke 15:11-32). This marvelous story reveals the heart of God to men, revealing that with unfailing love he waits to welcome every repentant soul. The parable of the Pharisee and publican suggests a similar fact (Luke 18:9-14). The publican, conscious of his sinfulness and unworthiness, prayed for God's forgiveness and received it.

Missionaries go to every part of the world with the knowledge that God does care for men and is ready in compassion to forgive all, no matter how unworthy, who will turn to him.

Jesus Adequate for Man's Needs

There were certain illustrations in parables used by Jesus which may be noted. Among these are the lifting up by Moses of the serpent in the wilderness (John 3:14), typifying the crucifixion, and his references to himself as the Bread of life, the Water of life, the Door of the sheepfold, the Good Shepherd, and the Vine. All of these have relevance for missions, as they suggest values available to every man.

In certain parables, Jesus pointed up not only the necessity of preparation for life after death but the consequences of failure to make this preparation. The parable of the rich fool (Luke 12:13-21) shows the folly of one who puts all his emphasis on the present and considers life to consist only of material possessions. The parable of the cruel vine dressers, or wicked tenants, in which Jesus suggests that he himself is the Messiah (Matt. 21:33-41; Mark 12:1-9; Luke 20:9-16) contains the acknowledgment even by those who heard Jesus that only judgment could be expected by men who reject the owner of the vineyard and fail in their stewardship. The parables of the wedding garment (Matt. 22:11-13), of excuses made by those invited to a banquet (Luke 14:15-24), of the wise and foolish virgins (Matt. 25:1-13), and the wise and foolish builders (Matt. 7:24-27), all suggest similar lessons of universal significance. In the unforgettable parable of the rich man and Lazarus (Luke 16:10-30), the veil is lifted to let us glimpse the future and see the consequences to a person who does not prepare for the life to come. Millions are dying every day, even as millions are being born. The estate of those destined to pass through the gate of death must ever be of concern to those who know the Lord of life. This, too, is a burden of missions.

God Seeks Man Continually

In the parables of the lost sheep (Luke 15:1-7) and the lost coin (Luke 15:8-10), Jesus taught that God is ever taking the initiative in seeking men. From the day Adam fell, when God sought him, saying, "Where art thou?" (Gen. 3:9) until now, his compassion has continued to reach out for men. God is "not willing that any should perish" (2 Peter 3:9), but that all should come to the knowledge of life. The diligence of the shepherd searching for his one lost sheep, and of the woman looking for her lost silver piece suggests how God keeps on in his search for sinful men.

His followers who would be like him must obviously also be concerned, as is he, to find those who are lost. They will rejoice, too, as does the shepherd over the sheep, the woman over the coin, the father over the prodigal son, when the lost are found.

God Is Impartial

One of the most difficult of all the parables is that of the laborers and the hours (Matt. 20:1-16). This parable seems to teach the impartiality of God. Although God has chosen Israel as an instrument to bring blessing to all nations, Christ declared in the parable of the rejected cornerstone (Matt. 21:42-46) that God was not partial to that nation. "The kingdom of God shall be taken from you," he warned, "and given to a nation bringing forth the fruits thereof." When people make a true response to him, they may be assured of God's response to them. Gentiles, as well as the Jews, who "bring forth fruits" are acceptable alike to him.

Sometimes one parable is built on another. This is true of the parables regarding the wicked husbandmen and the one concerning the rejected cornerstone (Matt. 21:33-41; Matt. 21:42-46). Another instance is that of the parable of the great feast with the added parable about the wedding garment (Matt. 22:1-14). In this parable, servants were finally sent into the highways and hedges to invite the poor, the maimed, the blind, and the lame (Luke 14:15-24). Matthew says those first invited had made light of the feast and had gone their own ways.

The story suggests that, whatever the excuse one gives for not accepting the invitation so graciously extended to the banquet table of the Lord, the results are the same. He commits spiritual suicide. God's grace is of such depths, however, that the door of his mercy remains open to all who will come. The following parable of the wedding garment indicates that inside the banquet hall is found one who responded to the invitation the wrong way. It is possible to make light of God's invitation by attempting to come on our own terms.

God's Terms Prevail

The lesson seems to be that one cannot enter the kingdom on his own terms, nor be saved by his own preferences. "The call is to all, but there must be the wedding garment" (Morgan). This parable ends with the awesome command: "Cast out into outer darkness; there shall be weeping and gnashing of teeth" (Matt. 8:12). Thus the fact of judgment is introduced. Jesus once remarked: "Many will say to me in that day, Lord, Lord, have we not . . . then will I profess unto them, I never knew you: depart from me" (Matt. 7:22-23). This warning, to be sure has significance for missions, both at home and abroad. The trouble with the greater part of the world is, not that they do not want to attend the "banquet," or inherit all God has promised, but they want to attend it on their own terms.

Three other parables also disclose the judgment and final separation of men: the parables of the tares (Matt. 13:24-46), the dragnet (Matt. 13:47-50), and the sheep and the goats (Matt. 25:31-46). In the first of these, the explanation of Jesus contains a phrase of key significance. It is "the field is the world." The wheat and the tares exist together in the world. The time will come, however, when a separation will take place. Though it is difficult now to tell the difference between the wheat and the tares, ultimately the true nature of each will be revealed. Jesus concludes this awesome parable with the warning: "The Son of man shall send forth his angels, and they shall gather out of his kingdom all things that offend, and them which do iniquity; and shall cast them into a furnace of fire: there shall be wailing and gnashing of teeth. Then shall the righteous shine forth as the sun in the kingdom of their Father. Who hath ears to hear, let him hear." (Matt. 13:41-43). Christ's parable of the dragnet discloses the nature and time of judgment. This parable concludes: "So shall it be at the end of the world: the angels shall come forth, and sever the wicked from among the just, and shall cast them into the furnace of fire: there shall be wailing and gnashing of teeth" (Matt. 13:49-50.)

The third of these parables is even clearer and more impressive. In it Jesus depicts the great scene of judgment when the sheep are gathered on the right hand and the goats on the left before "the Son of man shall come in his glory" (Matt. 25:31). Here it is clear that Jesus foresaw all nations and peoples as included in this final judgment. It is not the church or the spiritual nation with which the judge is concerned, but all the nations or peoples of the world. Great ethical and social responsibilities are suggested, to be sure, by this parable.

The Judgment Reveals What Man Is

The importance of what men actually are and not what they assume themselves to be is also declared. Some *are* sheep; others *are* goats. As G. Campbell Morgan wisely says: "The nations are not treated on the basis of race, or of political position, or occupation, or achievement, or failure and disaster. They are divided into sheep and goats, a division of the nations, a new separation. The old national lines are removed before the King: to his right and left hand, sheep and goats." It is evident, moreover, from the parable that the judgment here made is final and eternal.

Whatever else one may learn from the above parable he should not escape its meaning for missions. The whole world and every man in it is seen in this parable to await the hour of final judgment. Only those who are truly "the sheep of his pasture" are prepared for the glorious welcome, "Come, ye blessed of my Father, inherit the kingdom prepared for you from the foundation of the world" (Matt. 25:34). Such an awesome fact as this is a sufficient motivation for all who know Christ to desire a part in extending his glorious invitation to every man in all the earth, and persuading men to accept.

6—Missions in the Sermon on the Mount

Matthew 5:1 to 8:1; Luke 6:17-49

Seldom, if ever, is the Sermon on the Mount considered to teach anything of particular missionary relevance. An examination of the Sermon on the Mount, however, does establish Christ's missionary message. Not only is the sermon given great prominence, at least by Matthew, in the Gospels, but also it is the most extensive of the recorded sermons of the Master. Hence it would seem logical that if the Lord had a worldwide scope in his purpose, there would be some evidence of this in the Sermon on the Mount. And it is there.

Evidence may be found, for example, even in the Beatitudes which introduce the sermon. Here reference is made to "the kingdom of heaven." Christ had already said he came to preach the good news of the kingdom (Matt. 4:23). In the sermon he describes the kind of life expected from subjects of the kingdom. Entrance to it is assured all who are "poor in spirit" and are hence conscious of their spiritual need and mourn to have that need filled; who are meek and humble and who hunger and thirst after righteousness; who show mercy, seek purity of heart, endeavor to be peacemakers, and are willing to be persecuted for righteousness sake. Indeed, "theirs is the kingdom of heaven" (Matt. 5:10).

To the listening disciples, Jesus went on to say: "Ye are the salt of the earth, . . . ye are the light of the world" (Matt. 5:13-14). Those who are true subjects of that heavenly realm become as essential and meaningful among men as salt to the earth and as light to the world. Salt was then especially prized for its healing, preserving, and purifying powers. Its penetrating and self-giving qualities may also have been in the thought of Christ. Light was known to be essential to the natural world and a source of life.

A Missionary Sermon

It appears that very early in the public ministry of our Lord he defined the kind of life necessary if men would be useful in the world. One cannot truly and completely fulfil the commissions of our Lord unless he takes heed also to what is disclosed here (Matt. 4:17).

What many Christians seem to overlook is that in the task of being witnesses or missionaries in the world the first concern is not what they should *do,* but what they should *be.* The true witness of Christ, however, is both to *be* and to *do* something. His life is to express likeness to the King himself. Responsibility does not stop here, though, for Christ also said: "As my Father hath sent me, even so *send* I you" (John 20:21 author's italics).

If men are to be used of God in changing the world, let them give first thought to what they *are,* to the necessity of being "salt" and "light," and then to what they are to do. Salt loses itself for the sake of the "other." Men do not remark in eating cake, "How good the salt is," but "How good the cake is." Christ urges letting one's light shine before men "that they may *see your good works,* and glorify your Father which is in heaven" (Matt. 5:16 author's italics.) "In our era," once remarked the late Dag Hammerskjold, "the road to holiness necessarily passes through the world of action."

A Christian Is Salt and Light

In relationship to the missionary task, what Christians are is of crucial importance. What they are, however, is revealed largely in what they do. What they do, of course, involves a great deal more than mere verbal witness. To proclaim the gospel or to engage in personal soul-winning is extremely important, but what one is and what he does still speak more loudly than what he says.

Merely to be "good"—though highly important—is clearly in itself not enough. Findley Edge is right when he says: "It is true there are things that Christians should not do, but these things do not constitute the highest expression of the Christian life. Christianity is fundamentally a positive religion. It must now be said that the primary task of Christianity is not simply to make people 'good'; its task is to make people Christian. The church errs when it comes to feel that leading people to live good, clean, moral lives is its ultimate task. Yet many church leaders are satisfied with this mistaken view. For him to accept his mission and to fulfil his ministry in the world is thus the distinctive aspect of the Christian life." The view here stated seems well founded in what Christ said regarding salt and light. In these two masterful figures of speech, both the *being* and the *doing* of the Christian life are inseparably related. The objective of each, moreover, has "the earth" or "world" in view.

Attitudes Are Significant

Jesus pointed up in the Sermon on the Mount that he did not come to destroy the law or the prophets but to fulfil them. He revealed, moreover, that in fulfilling them, those who did not "exceed" the righteousness of the Scribes and Pharisees could in no wise enter the kingdom of heaven. To exceed the righteousness of these keepers of the law, however, requires more than mere literal observance of the law. The law, for example, forbids one to kill; but Christ said that one who is angry with his brother is in danger of judgment. He added that one's right relationship with his offended brother is more important than the making of his stewardship gift at the altar (Matt. 5:21-26). Not merely is one forbidden to commit adultery, but the very existence of lust in the mind makes one guilty. The law may allow retaliation, but he who would follow Christ must be willing to go the "second mile," to give his "cloak, also," Indeed, one is to love his enemies and pray for those who persecute him. "What do ye more than others?" (Matt. 5:7) Jesus pointedly asked. Must not both the life and the work of the Christian exceed even the best standards of the non-Christian?

A true follower of Christ is not to make his major investment in the treasures of earth but in the treasures of heaven. Knowing that God who cares even for the birds of the heavens and the grass of the field cares for him, one is to put first things first by seeking first he kingdom and his righteousness. If one is to be a rectifier of others' faults, he is first to make sure that he has rectified his own: "How wilt thou say to thy brother, Let me pull out the mote out of thine eye; and behold, the beam is in thine own eye?" (Matt. 7:4).

All the teachings set down in the Sermon on the Mount are important considerations for one who would responsibly fulfil his mission as a Christian.

In a day when all the world knows what all the rest of the world is doing, failure on the part of Christians to apply the teachings of Christ to their daily living will be well known to those they would win. Instead of letting their shortcomings glare embarrassingly in the eyes of the world, it becomes more imperative than ever that they remember the Master's admonition: "Let your light so shine before men, that they may see your good works, and glorify your Father which is in heaven" (Matt. 5:16).

The Worldwide Kingdom

In two particular sections of the Sermon on the Mount, the one relating to the Lord's Prayer (Matt. 6:5-15) and the one relating to the Golden Rule (Matt. 7:7-12), the whole world is so distinctly in view as to give these passages special meaning for missions. "Thy kingdom come. Thy will be done, in earth as it is in heaven" (Matt. 6:10). The conception here of the coming of the kingdom, of course, has worldwide dimensions.

Followers of Christ are to be concerned to see his will done in all the earth. In interpreting this part of the prayer one commentator in fact says: "Thus are we taught to pray, and consequently to expect and to labor, for the extension of Christ's kingdom over the whole world." In harmony with this is the Great Commission (Matt. 28:19-20); and hence the missionary imperatives for preaching the gospel to the heathen, and to the spiritually destitute everywhere. Every Christian in some sense should be a missionary. Matthew Henry believes "thy kingdom come; thy will be done" means "Let the gospel be preached to all and embraced by all; let all be brought to subscribe to the record God has given his Word concerning his Son, and to embrace him as their Saviour and Sovereign. Let the bounds of the gospel-church be enlarged, the kingdom of the world be made Christ's kingdom, and all men become subjects to it, and live as becomes their character."

This matchless prayer supports what Christ had preached and had taught his disciples to preach regarding the kingdom. Through all the centuries since Adam, God had sought by love and patient persuasion to lead men into the spiritual realm of renewed personal relationship with him. The unceasing prayer and passion of true followers of Christ are ever to look toward this goal.

The Golden Rule Is Missionary

Another expression in the Sermon on the Mount seems also to have significant overtones, if not direct implications, for missions.

It is what has been called the Golden Rule: "Therefore all things whatsoever ye would that men should do to you, do ye even so to them: for this is the law and the prophets" (Matt. 7:12). This rule, of course, was set down to regulate all our conduct and all our relationships.

If, however, we are to *do* unto others what we would have them do unto us, there is an ocean's depth of responsibility placed upon us. When the Golden Rule is laid down by the side of the fact of the lostness of mankind without Christ and the further fact that the great masses of lost will never hear the gospel unless someone who knows it bears the message to them, then the obligation that it lays upon us is staggering.

Those who recognize the importance of the Golden Rule can never be comfortable when hearing such pointed questions as: "How then shall they call on him in whom they have not believed? and how shall they believe in him of whom they have not heard? and how shall they hear without a preacher?" (Rom. 10:14).

How can we who have discovered the riches of Christ's salvation and fellowship imagine ourselves in the state of the great hoards who have never even heard of him, and avoid the obligation the Golden Rule lays upon us? Its demands indeed in this light are almost the equivalent of those of the Great Commission itself.

Doing the Sayings of the Lord

Dr. George W. Truett is quoted once to have said: "The consequences to a church without a mission spirit are so direful that it becomes a hospital; unless it is converted, God removes its candlestick and then it becomes a graveyard. Our only safety is that we give ourselves to the supreme purpose and passion of Christianity."

The great Sermon on the Mount declares, near its conclusion: "Not every one that saith unto me, Lord, Lord, shall enter into the kingdom of heaven; but he that doeth the will of my Father which is in heaven" (Matt. 7:21). The only way one can truly make Christ Lord is, not by a mere verbal affirmation, but by doing what he wills. Affirming this truth, the Sermon on the Mount concludes with a reminder that whoever both hears and does God's will is likened unto one who builds his house upon a rock where it withstands the tests of time and storms.

7 —Missions and Christ's Compassion

See selected passages in text.

In a sense it may be correctly said that Christian missions is the consequence of Christ's compassion. Looking upon the multitudes, he saw them as sheep without a shepherd. His whole inner being stirred with a desire to help. The Scriptures say simply that he was moved with compassion.

The dictionary definition of "compassion" as being a feeling of sympathy or of pity is too mild to carry the full New Testament idea. The Greek word translated "compassion" referred to bowels, the viscera, or the heart, and carried the idea of deep inward feeling, or even of a pain of the heart. In a manner then compassion could be called "a pain of love." It is more than mere "feeling within." It is love and sympathy of such depth as almost to cause a painful compulsion to do something about the condition one sees or senses.

"God so loved . . . that he gave" (John 3:16) is the immortal explanation lying back of our salvation. Divine compassion became love in action, love which led to the *event* of Christ's birth, death, and resurrection.

"Compassion" is a "human" word, which implies a physical response. How then may it be used appropriately of Christ? It may help us to understand if we recall that the "Word was made flesh" (John 1:1), the divine Son became also the *man* Christ Jesus. God in Christ bridged the gulf between himself and man by taking on himself our flesh. "We have not an high priest which cannot be touched with the feeling of our infirmities" (Heb. 4:15). A word such as compassion helps us to sense how the Son of God in the flesh actually felt about man's need.

To Christ, the sight of need of any kind—physical, mental, or spiritual—stirred the depths of his sympathy and pity and drew out of him a compelling desire to relieve the need. We read: "When he saw the multitudes, he was moved with compassion on them" (Matt. 9:36). Again, "And Jesus went forth, and saw a great multitude, and was moved with compassion toward them, and he healed their sick" (Matt. 14:14). And again, "Then Jesus called his disciples unto him, and said, I have compassion on the multitudes" (Matt. 15:32). He told, also, of the father of the unworthy prodigal son, who when the son was a great way off saw him "and had compassion, and ran, and fell on his neck, and kissed him" (Luke 15:20). Jesus suggested by the story that the Heavenly Father responds toward those who repent as this father responded to the returning prodigal; that is, with compassion and love.

Compassion over Physical Affliction

Two blind men sitting by a wayside, on hearing that Christ was approaching, cried out, "Have mercy on us, O Lord, thou son of David" (Matt. 20:30). The impatient multitude rebuked them, ordering them to be silent; but the men kept on crying for mercy. "Jesus stood still, and called them, and said, What will ye that I shall do unto you?" (Matt. 20:32). It is noted: "Jesus had compassion on them, and touched their eyes: and immediately their eyes received sight, and they followed him" (Matt. 20:34). Thus the New Testament story runs, in instance after instance. More than one reason may have motivated Christ in what he did, but it seems obvious that the basic reason for his healing work was his own inner compassion. The world's untold suffering still cries out for Christian compassion.

Compassion for the Hungry

Not only physical afflictions, such as described above, however, wrung from Jesus a compassionate response. Hunger, too, concerned him. The multitudes who followed him for days at a time also experienced his compassion. In at least two instances, the feeding of the five thousand and of the four thousand, we have evidence of his concern about hunger. One wonders what he would say if he were addressing us now when millions still are starving. Jesus' own reason for feeding the hungry is set down by Mark (Mark 6:35-46; 8:1-9). "I have compassion on the multitude, because they have now been with me three days, and have nothing to eat: and if I send them away fasting to their own houses, they will faint by the way: for divers of them came from far" (Mark 8:2-3). Many coming from distant places had been so absorbed in what he was saying and so stirred with hope by him that they kept following to the point of exhaustion. Jesus, knowing this, was moved with compassion toward them.

Missionaries and mission boards have often felt similar compassion for the hungry and destitute in many parts of the world and have usually been in the forefront of those who sought to relieve starvation and bring new hope to the destitute.

Compassion for the Sorrowing and Distraught

But physical needs, whether hunger or deeper physical afflictions, were not the only concerns of Christ. His compassion went out also to people in sorrow, or in mental anguish. It was true, as we have seen, of the widow at Nain. It was true of the sisters, Martha and Mary. On their way to the tomb of their brother Lazarus, Jesus was so moved by their sorrow that he, too, wept. How often since have others been comforted and given reassurance in times of sorrow, as were these sisters, by remembering this scene. When it is recalled that Christ knew he could and would soon raise Lazarus, yet he wept, one begins to see how deeply pained he was by the sorrow of these sisters.

Compassion over Intellectual and Spiritual Needs

Jesus made it a part of his ministry to bring relief to physical need and sorrow. Even more, however, he was distressed about men's mental and spiritual needs. Mark recorded significantly: "And Jesus, when he came out, saw much people, and was moved with compassion toward them, because they were as sheep not having a shepherd: and he began to teach them many things" (Mark 6:34).

Matthew added that further reason for the Master's compassion was "because they fainted [were distressed], and were scattered abroad" (Matt. 9:36). The picture here made by the original text is that of a people "harassed, importuned, bewildered by those who should have taught them; hindered from entering the kingdom of heaven, ladened with the burdens which the Pharisees laid upon . . . [They were as men cast down and prostrate on the ground . . . in a state of mental dejection]" (Robertson). Neither Rome, with its heathen worship of emperor or of idols, nor Israel offered hope. Confused and caught between conflicting forces, religious and political, the multitude was in a tragic condition, not greatly unlike that of the masses of this day.

They needed to be taught, and Jesus knew this. Scattered abroad as sheep that had no shepherd, they had become wearied and were distrustful of their religious leaders, wandering and ready to follow anyone who would promise relief. Jesus taught them the truth about themselves, about God, about their need of salvation, and about the way of hope. How greatly needed is this same kind of instruction for the masses now suffering the same disadvantage and tragic need. This is one of the highly important reasons why our mission boards have sent Christian teachers and have established schools.

In a recent conference where representatives of Christian colleges from missions fields around the world were assembled, the writer was privileged to meet, and to hear reports directly from national presidents and deans of these Christian schools. It was an inspiring experience. He was assured that, in large measure, the only valid hope that the flourishing new nations will reject communism and follow Christ is that most of the education the young have received until recently has been provided by mission schools and Christian teachers.

To whatever degree the future is uncertain, one of the reasons may be that we have not established enough schools and sent enough devoted Christian teachers to non-Christian lands. Jesus' teaching, of course, had as its ultimate goal meeting the spiritual needs of all who heard. He apparently considered the needs of the soul more important than the needs of the body. This is suggested by his forgiving the paralytic his sins before he healed him. He thus appears to have given priority to the inner spiritual condition of the man (see Mark 2:1-12).

Compassion for Sinners

Jesus' compassion always reached out to people who were victims of sin. An example was the woman taken in adultery. Tenderly forgiving her, Jesus firmly charged her, "Go, and sin no more" (John 8:1-11). Another woman called a sinner (Luke 7:36-50) was assured after her repentance and expression of faith in and gratitude to Christ for his compassion on her: "Thy sins are forgiven . . . Thy faith hath saved thee; go in peace" (Luke 7:48,50). So it was. Wherever there was genuine grief for sin and a desire to be freed from its enslavement, Jesus responded in compassion. He wanted all who had such a sense of sin and guilt to know the mercies to be found in God. "In the last day," John told us, "that great day of the feast, Jesus stood and cried, saying, If any man thirst, let him come unto me, and drink. He that believeth on me, as the Scripture hath said, out of his belly shall flow rivers of living water" (John 7:37-38). This was a universal invitation. It encompassed every man who *thirsted.* The same invitation is echoed in Revelation: "And the Spirit and the bride say, Come. And let him that heareth say, Come. And let him that is athirst come. And *whosoever will,* let him take the water of life freely" (Rev. 22:17 author's italics). Jesus explicitly invited all men to him saying, "Come unto me, *all* ye that labour and are heavy laden, and I will give you rest" (Matt. 11:28 author's italics).

The compassion of Christ reaches as far and as deep as the needs of man extend. Those who would be like him cannot stop short of similar compassion. Dr. Carl F. H. Henry, chairman of the Berlin World Congress on Evangelism in the summer of 1966 and former editor of *Christianity Today,* has said, "The decline of evangelistic compassion is the most crucial matter facing Christendom today." This is true of missions also, for missions is basically only evangelism written large. However much hardness of heart among men and rejection of divine love was shown, Jesus still cared. This he disclosed in that profoundly moving scene when he entered Jerusalem on Sunday before the crucifixion and beheld the city whose hardness of heart had shut the door of hope for its people. He longed to give them hope and salvation, but they had not heeded. Yet he wept over the city (see Luke 19:41).

The lesson for us who are Christ's seems clearly obvious. It is that, if we would be truly his, our concern must never cease. Regardless of the response given, our compassionate desire must ever be to see men saved. Here lies, in great measure, the motive and the dynamic for missions both at home and abroad. Here lies also the central purpose for the mission strategy of establishing churches to witness and to serve in all parts of the earth.

8—Missions and the Main Needs of Man

See selected passages in text.

Christian missions is founded upon the conviction that in Christ, and in Christ alone, all the deepest needs of man may be adequately met. But what are these needs? Man is a physical, intellectual, social, and spiritual being. That he is more than flesh and blood, more than merely a physical creature, both the Bible and reason testify. Yet he does have a physical nature the demands of which must be satisfied. Having such, he obviously also has in common with all living creatures certain basic natural needs. This, of course, God knows better than man. "Your heavenly Father knoweth," said Jesus, "that ye have need of these things" (Matt. 6:32). Jesus was not an ascetic who ignored the natural needs of the body. He not only attended banquets and other gatherings such as wedding feasts, eating and drinking what was placed before him, but also he had compassion on the hungry and more than once sought to relieve their distress. This leads us to believe the hungry everywhere are his missionary concern, and so must be ours.

Illness and physical disability were also of concern to Christ, as his ministry of healing so abundantly witnesses. This fact has warranted the effort of missionaries across the years to treat the sick, to relieve pain, and to make the lame whole.

Man's suffering is not confined to physical pain, for man is a psychological and social being, as well as a living creature. Injustice, oppression, and ignorance also plague him. As the Gospels repeatedly disclose, these conditions were also of deep concern to Christ. For instance, his shattering rebuke of those who "bind heavy burdens and grievous to be borne, and lay them on men's shoulders" (Matt. 23:4) gives telling evidence of how he felt. Missions then is rightly burdened over these things. The vastness in the world of such needs as these is staggering.

But after all of this is said, it must be added that Jesus apparently did not consider the physical needs of man, or even his social needs, to be supreme. "Life," he said, is "more than meat, and the body more than raiment" (Matt. 6:25). He taught, "A man's life consisteth not in the abundance of the things which he possesseth" (Luke 12:15). Missions is primarily concerned, therefore, over other things than meat, raiment, and possessions. Besides food and shelter, relief of hunger and suffering, undoing the bondage of injustice, oppression, and ignorance, what other universal needs do the Gospels teach should be the concern of Christians? What should motivate them to world missionary endeavor?

A System of Moral Values

Is not one of these needs an adequate system of moral values? This is surely not only one of the deepest needs of the ages but also one which is growing more acute. As the world's population increases, issues become increasingly serious. The complexity of life makes it often more difficult than ever to know what is right and wrong. Because of this difficulty much has been said in recent years about the need of a new morality. What is really needed is a new understanding or application of New Testament morality. It would seem that only by the finding and applying of moral values based on God's law can the world much longer endure.

No other moral system is comparable to that found in the New Testament. Instead of setting up mere codes of conduct, Jesus said, "I am the way, the truth" (John 14:6), and then showed men how to live. To the Mosiac commandments he added interpretations which literally filled them full of meaning for all ages. Much of the non-Christian world—including many of its religions—has been influenced in one way or another by Christian ethical teachings. To be sure, sometimes non-Christians have been appalled or offended by certain practices of people or nations considered Christian; but even this has been proof of the quality of the Christian moral standards. They would never have been appalled or offended had they not expected better conduct from those judged to be Christian. And they expected this because of what they knew Christ to be and to have taught.

A Japanese Buddhist says: "As a Christian morality, I find nothing to add to Christ's saying, 'none is good save one, even God.' Here is the inexhaustible fountain of Christian morality. All moralities flow out of this one and only source."

The Way of Forgiveness

Another fundamental need of man is forgiveness. This need is so great that guilt has been a subject of deepest interest to many. Some appear to assume that if all inhibitions and religious ideas of right and wrong could be removed, guilt would vanish. This is naive. Guilt reaches too deep into the nature of man for such easy removal. It can be relieved only by a knowledge of forgiveness. "Guilt," says the famous Swiss psychiatrist, Dr. Paul Tournier, "is therefore a religious problem which interests theologians, a social problem which interests psychologists. But it does not let itself be dissected. It is a human problem, a form of suffering peculiar to man, and of concern to the doctor because his vocation is the relief of all suffering." This form of suffering was also of concern to Christ. His assurance, "thy sins be forgiven thee" (Matt. 9:2), is among the most blessed ever given. Who could count the masses in the world who suffer from a sense of guilt?

Guilt cannot forever be forgotten. It cannot be removed by scalpel or dispelled by psychological insights. The only way to get rid of it is to find forgiveness. In none other but God alone can abiding assurance of forgiveness be obtained. The prayer of Christ on the cross, "Father, forgive them; for they know not what they do" (Luke 23:24), includes every man and reassures all that they can have forgiveness.

John, who apparently witnessed Christ's death on the cross, declared, "If we confess our sins, he is faithful and just to forgive us our sins, and to cleanse us from all unrighteousness" (1 John 1:9).

Jesus taught us to forgive each other. Without this, he said, we cannot hope to obtain God's forgiveness. For men not to learn the way of forgiveness toward one another is to add increasingly to the bedlam of hate and tension in our world. Truly to be able to forgive, one must learn the way of divine forgiveness. This is one of the messages Christians are surely appointed to proclaim.

Dr. Tournier says: "Our privilege as Christians is to know that we are forgiven, and that forgiveness reaches us through Jesus Christ."

Peace Within and Without

Another basic need of man is reconciliation. He needs somehow to find reconciliation with himself, with his fellowman, and above all with God. The world is full of tension, separation, alienation, and estrangement. Much of this exists because of a problem in each heart itself. When one is not truly reconciled within, that is, at peace, he is likely to be an agent of estrangement. How can one find reconciliation? "Only the holy love of God can burn the sin to ashes, so that it is no more," writes William Manson. "This redeeming love of God is what the Christian church sees brought to light in the passion and death of Jesus Christ."

Thus peace is brought to the heart, a peace "which passeth all understanding" (Phil. 4:7). Out of this peace come the influences that lead one to become himself a peacemaker, an instrument of reconciliation. The disciples found it so and thus were moved to fulfil Christ's commission to be "fishers of men" (Matt. 4:19). Paul so understood it, recognizing that "God was in Christ, reconciling the world unto himself" (2 Cor. 5:19). He then declared, as he saw the glory of his own task: "And hath committed unto us the word of reconciliation" (2 Cor. 5:19). He added, apparently with a sense of awe and wonder: "Now then we are ambassadors for Christ, as though God did beseech you by us: we pray you in Christ's stead, be ye reconciled to God" (2 Cor. 5:20).

Among the deepest needs any man can know are first to find peace or reconciliation within, and then to obtain reconciliation with his fellows. But neither of these is abidingly possible without peace with God.

Love: a Basic Need of Man

A further basic need of man is love. We are told that most criminals come from backgrounds where love has been absent. If love on the part of both husband and wife is deep enough for each other, no obstacle, short of death itself, can break their marriage bond. Paul could say, "And now abideth faith, hope, charity, these three; but the greatest of these is charity" (1 Cor. 13:13).

In all the earth people yearn to be loved. This yearning is as natural as the cry of the body for food. Love has reached its highest revelation in God's gift of Christ. Jesus declared: "God so loved the world [that is, all men] that he gave his only begotten Son, that whosoever believeth in him should not perish, but have everlasting life" (John 3:16). And it was Christ's own love toward men that led him to the cross and to lay down his life there for man's redemption.

Every soul—no matter what his circumstances, race, or nationality—can thus be assured that God loves him. He may not be able to answer all the questions with which he is confronted or to understand all his problems, but he can know that God is love.

Referring to his own death on the cross, Jesus declared: "Greater love hath no man than this, that a man lay down his life for his friends" (John 15:13). Missionaries rejoice to proclaim the glorious good news of his love to all the earth. They also persuade men to "walk in love, as Christ also hath loved us, and hath given himself for us an offering and a sacrifice to God for a sweetsmelling savour" (Eph. 5:2).

The apostle Paul's missionary burden arose in large part out of his dedication to the biblical view of love for men in need. "[He] evidently regarded the proclamation of the gospel to the unbeliever as an indispensable element in the Christian manifestation of love," observes an eminent writer. "But Christian love is only half biblical," this writer adds, "when it deteriorates into a concern only for souls of men and is indifferent to the needs of the body. What believer ministers to himself only in this way?" On the other hand, the writer further remarks: "It is scarcely biblical at all when it [love] degenerates into a mere humanistic concern for the social side of life to the total neglect of the life of the spirit (2 Cor. 4:2). The believer is obligated to bring into the life of another every blessing that lies within his power to communicate." All of this, God's love will long also to do for all others.

The Source of Spiritual Life

Finally, the deepest need of man is spiritual life. This is that kind of life to which Jesus referred when he said: "Ye will not come to me, that ye might have life" (John 5:40), or, "I am come that they might have life, and that they might have it more abundantly" (John 10:10). This life is found in Christ who declared, "I am . . . the life" (John 14:6). For one to live spiritually, he must find Christ, the only source of spiritual life.

Repentance toward God leads to forgiveness, and forgiveness brings reconciliation with God. In that state of reconciliation one finds peace and discovers life—life abundant and eternal. In this experience he comes to know also, in all its riches and wonder, the inexhaustible and ineffable love of God.

With adequate moral standards then to live by, assurance of forgiveness and removal of the pain of guilt, reconciliation with God, and a convincing assurance that God loves him in spite of his unworthiness, man will discover his deepest needs being met. No matter what the storms of life or how great the turbulence of the times, he can thereafter have a sure foundation to stand on. Having found Christ and spiritual life through him, he now has also something eternally significant to stand for, the making known of Christ to others. Here, too, is the chain of events which leads to the setting apart of every Christian.

9—Missions and the Ministry of the Holy Spirit

See selected passages in text.

Without the Holy Spirit, not only would the work of missions be impossible, but also the whole missionary enterprise would never have existed. "Worldwide missions constitute a divine enterprise," says Robert Hall Glover, "directed not merely from heaven but by the Holy Spirit in person sent down to earth for that purpose. And since he was to be the Commander-in-chief of the great campaign, its inception must await his arrival." The Spirit, however, is more than the Commander-in-chief of the missionary enterprise. He is literally its life and its power.

Dr. Glover thinks the Holy Spirit has a twofold ministry in relationship to Christian missions: (1) enduement of the individual worker with spiritual power, and (2) the supreme command and direction of the entire enterprise. Historically, it was he, of course, who effected the tremendous event of the incarnation and the virgin birth (Matt. 1:18-20); gave assurance as to the identity of Christ as the eternal Word, the only son of God; inspired many to recognize Jesus at his birth as the Anointed One; and bore special witness to Christ at his baptism. Acts and other books of the New Testament reveal many other services he rendered.

The Work of the Holy Spirit in the Witness of the Disciples

We cannot escape the obvious conclusion that Christ founded his church upon the Great Commission as its "charter of incorporation." The church would be helpless in the world, however, without the presence and power of the Spirit. The church has no alternative but to be a witnessing church in all the world if it would be true to its charter. Its witness is given, of course, in word and in deed. Strength to bear this witness is given through the Holy Spirit.

The Holy Spirit "abides" within the believer and the church. Jesus assured his disciples: "I will pray the Father, and he shall give you another Comforter, that he may abide with you for ever" (John 14:16). The Comforter, of course, is the Holy Spirit, the third person of the Trinity. He takes up his dwelling in the lives of those who have given themselves to Christ and in the church which is the body of Christ.

The Greek word used for "comforter" is *parakleton,* which no single English word quite expresses. This explains why the word is variously rendered as Comforter, Counselor, Helper, Intercessor, Advocate, Strengthener, and Standby. These names are suggestive of what the Spirit means to the Christian. He gives guidance, enlightenment, strength, comfort, courage, and assurance. He is also an intercessor, advocate. He gives the assurance needed by the believer, that he is a child of God. Paul reminded us, "The Spirit itself beareth witness with our spirit, that we are the children of God" (Rom. 8:16). He helps us moreover, in our infirmities, said Paul in Romans 8:26. Thus even in our frail attempts to pray, we have a helper who never fails us. "But the Spirit of him that raised up Jesus from the dead dwell in you, he that raised up Christ from the dead shall also quicken your mortal bodies by his Spirit that dwelleth in you" (Rom. 8:11). Did the apostle here mean that the Holy Spirit revives and renews our mortal bodies that they may be refreshed for his service? Many a missionary whose labor has gone beyond the limits of normal human strength has felt so. How reassuring it is, moreover, to know that in the ignorance and weakness which so characterize our praying, the Holy Spirit understands and makes intercession for us.

The Holy Spirit performs a constant ministry of teaching in the life of the believer and the church (see John 14:26). The Spirit gives assurance in the first place that the disciples would be afforded divine guidance in their communication of what they had learned from Christ. In the Spirit's special ministry to the disciples, he would teach them the meaning of all Jesus had taught and done and would bring to their remembrance the things they needed to recall and to set down as well. This ministry of the Spirit, we believe, has not ended. He continues to perform this service among those who are committed to Christ. Thus they do not depend alone on their own wisdom but also seek the guidance of the authoritative Word the Spirit has inspired.

The Spirit is ready to assist every humble and diligent student of the Word to understand more of the depth, meaning, and riches of the Word, and to empower him to share what he has discovered with others. The missionary then—and every Christian ought to be missionary—has a teacher always beside him (or dwelling within him). "Howbeit when he, the Spirit of truth, is come, he will guide you into all truth: for he shall not speak of himself; but whatsoever he shall hear, that shall he speak: and he will shew you things to come" (John 16:13).

God's truth, of course, is so vast and deep we would never presume to know it all in this life. Yet we can be growing constantly in that knowledge. The Spirit is striving thus to guide us. The truth to which Jesus referred may be even broader than that contained in the Scriptures themselves, though it surely includes this. It may be the truth regarding the nature and needs of men, the techniques of service, or the plans and program by which to reach men. But it is and will always be the truth somehow related to man's need and God's exalted purpose for him. In strategy of our missions agencies, the founding of churches, the work of promoting missions in our local churches, and the many other ways, the Spirit still wants to guide us. He may also point to specific fields of need or areas to which our ignorance and prejudice may have blinded us. The Holy Spirit led Paul to Macedonia instead of to Bithynia.

The Holy Spirit provides power for the worldwide witness of the church. Dr. H. Cornell Goerner has written, "It is a grave responsibility to be a steward of the gospel of salvation." Indeed, it is. It is so grave that none could bear it were it not for the help of the Holy Spirit. Yet if we need evidence of what the Holy Spirit can do with ordinary men, all we need to do is read the first two chapters of the book of Acts. The 120 in the upper room were given power even to use languages that every man understood; that is, a power of communication which enabled them to reach the heart of every hearer.

The Holy Spirit affords varying gifts to believers. "Now there are diversities of gifts, but the same Spirit" (1 Cor. 12:4), Paul said. (See 1 Cor. 12:7-11.) These various gifts, dedicated to

Christ, complement each other as the various parts of a body, the whole. The point he expressed is, not only the fact of these gifts and their variety, but also the responsibility of their possession. We are to exercise them for the common good. Everyone is so blessed; he can assist somehow in the great world missions enterprise.

The Holy Spirit exercises supreme command in direction of the missionary enterprise. The reading of Acts—which could be called the Acts of the Holy Spirit—will reveal how the Spirit gave early Christians power for service and constantly pointed out their course of action. He not only directed them on the day of Pentecost but also guided those, such as Philip, who were scattered abroad by persecution in their continuing witness for Christ. Thus Philip's ministry in Samaria bore tremendous fruit. Thus his footsteps were guided to the Ethiopian eunuch, and his tongue was guided to interpret the Scriptures to this government official.

The Work of the Spirit in Relationship to the World

The ministry of the Holy Spirit is, not only to equip and direct Christians in their world task, but also to have a bearing upon the world.

There are at least three great areas of service the Holy Spirit performs in relationship to the world. The first is obviously to provide the world the witness of the church. The Holy Spirit moved upon the early church to appoint missionaries to the non-Christian world and from that day until this has been calling and thrusting out missionaries around the globe. Fifty percent of the world's population has not yet heard the gospel, but not because God does not want them saved. Neither is it because the Holy Spirit is not working to energize the church for the task. It is rather because either Christians have been less than willing to respond as needed, or the world has resisted or rejected the witness given it.

Yet another work of the Holy Spirit in relation to the world is his desire to provide all men with the Scriptures and also to assure them that he will use the Word of God to quicken into life all who will open their minds and hearts to him. One of the miracles of the ages is how God chose a variety of people over a period of hundreds of years to set down a revelation of such dependability that through it every reverent soul seeking to know God can find him. This truth has been proved so often as to be a self-evident truth. "It is the spirit," said Jesus, "that quickeneth; the flesh profiteth nothing: the words that I speak unto you, they are spirit, and they are life" (John 6:63).

The great convicting work of the Holy Spirit in behalf of the world is expressed clearly by Christ as follows: "When he [the Holy Spirit] is come, he will reprove the world of sin, and of righteousness, and of judgment: of sin, because they believed not on me; of righteousness, because I go to my Father, and ye see me no more; of judgment, because the prince of this world is judged" (John 16:8-11). In the deepest sense the world's hope rests upon this particular work of the Spirit. Never would men sense the need of a Saviour at all, or even know the seriousness of sin, were it not for the Spirit. They might recognize the evil in them as crime, maladjustment, or unsocial activity, but never as sin. Only the Holy Spirit can enlighten our eyes to see our inner need and wretchedness. He reveals, moreover, the horror of sin and its power. He points out the consequences, also, of what sin will do in one's life and awakens a yearning to be rid of its condemnation. The Holy Spirit often convicts men of sin through the witness of Christian men and women.

The Holy Spirit also enlightens men as to the nature and need of righteousness. He reveals that righteousness can be measured only in terms of one's relationship to God. The righteousness required, moreover, can be achieved only through the help of the Holy Spirit. In truth, without the laws God has set down there can be no such thing as righteousness, for without God and the standards he has revealed all other criteria for behavior would be only relative at best.

Finally, the Holy Spirit convicts men of judgment. He first enlightens them as to the nature and awfulness of sin and that they are sinners. As he further makes known the one eternal standard of righteousness existing in God himself, he arouses men also to see that judgment is inevitable. One cannot continue to sin and thus ignore his spiritual need and the demands of righteousness without coming sometime to a final judgment. All evil and all sin must ultimately meet a judgment which none can escape. This is a message of universal application. This the Holy Spirit speaks with convicting power.

10—Missions and the Meaning of the Cross

See selected passages in text.

All the world is gathered up in the cross. The best known text in the Bible is likely: "For God so loved the world, that he gave his only begotten Son, that whosoever believeth in him should not perish, but have everlasting life" (John 3:16). The giving emphasized here is the offering up of Christ on the cross.

Christians may disagree on many things, but the belief most commonly held among them is that the cross has a universality of value. Christ died for all. No study of the missionary message of the Bible would be adequate, therefore, if it did not deal seriously with the great and fundamental reality of what was done at Golgotha for all the world.

Professor Ralph Earle observes: "Calvary stands at the crossroads of human history. All the divine paths of the past led to it. All the divine paths of the present and future lead from it."

"All the sin of the ages," Dr. Earle further comments, "was placed on the heart of the sinless Son of God, as the racial representative of all humanity. From the cross salvation flows to every believing soul. This is the gospel, the greatest good news the world has ever heard."

"The death of Jesus on the cross has had a strange power," Miss Georgia Harkness rightly thinks, "to redeem men from sin and hopelessness because it was the death of no ordinary man, but of the Son of God. . . . His death has drawn men toward God because in it God himself was acting for our salvation."

Now let us look at some of the things the Bible itself says about the cross, noting especially the things which have significance for missions.

The Old Testament Foreview of the Cross

Many think that even in Genesis we have a foreshadowing of the cross. After the disobedience of Adam and Eve, God is recorded to have made the following judgment: "And I will put enmity between thee [the serpent] and the woman, and between thy seed and her seed; it shall bruise thy head, and thou shalt bruise his heel" (Gen. 3:15).

Psalm 22 seems much like a description of the agony of the cross and has caused some to wonder whether Jesus himself did not have this very Psalm in mind as he suffered there. He appears to at least have quoted from this Psalm in his cry: "My God, my God, why hast thou forsaken me?" (Psalm 22:1).

More than any other Old Testament book, Isaiah forecasts the sufferings of the cross and the purpose for which those sufferings were endured. Such passages as "And the Redeemer shall come to Zion, and unto them that turn from transgression in Jacob, saith the Lord" (Isa. 59:20), and "In all their affliction he was afflicted, and the angel of his presence saved them: in his love and in his pity he redeemed them; and he bare them, and carried them all the days of old" (Isa. 63:9), appear to have their chief fulfilment in the death of Christ. Though they may have had an earlier meaning for Israel, they apparently foreshadowed the cross itself.

The passage in Isaiah which most fully seems to show the agony of Calvary and its universal significance is the famous fifty-third chapter. The eloquence and majesty of this chapter are equaled only by its descriptive power. It is almost as lofty and as moving as the accounts of the crucifixion found in the Gospels themselves. Though some hold this passage spoke only of the role of Israel as a suffering servant, one is almost forced to think of the cross as he reads: "He is despised and rejected of men; a man of sorrows, and acquainted with grief: and we hid as it were our faces from him; he was despised, and we esteemed him not. Surely he hath borne our griefs, and carried our sorrows: . . . but he was wounded for our transgressions, he was bruised for our iniquities: . . . and with his stripes we are healed" (Isa. 53:3-5).

The universal purpose of the suffering here so poignantly depicted begins to appear as we read further: "All we like sheep have gone astray; we have turned every one to his own way; and the Lord hath laid on him the iniquity of us all" (Isa. 53:6).

Every man is in that picture! Everyone may find hope also in that assurance! In verse 11, we read that the agony described will have an effect upon many. In the last verse of the chapter it is said, "And he bare the sin of many" (Isa. 53:12). Many would be made righteous through the suffering described. Surely these assurances have value for all men.

Anticipations of the Cross at the Birth of Christ

When we turn to the pages of the New Testament, it becomes apparent the Old Testament promises of the one who would suffer for the redemption of many are fulfilled in Christ. Matthew reminds us that the Holy Spirit revealed to Joseph: "And she [Mary] shall bring forth a son, and thou shalt call his name Jesus [Saviour]: for he shall save his people from their sins" (Matt. 1:21). Zacharias was inspired to see that in the birth of Christ, God had "visited and redeemed his people" (Luke 1:68) and had "raised up a horn of salvation" (Luke 1:69). This had come about through the tender mercy of God, which mercy toward the world was as a sun rising (Luke 1:77-79).

Aging Simeon, when Mary brought Jesus to the Temple at the time of her purification, was moved to prophesy: "For mine eyes have seen thy salvation, which thou hast prepared before the face of all people; a light to lighten the Gentiles, and the glory of thy people Israel" (Luke 2:30-32). This remark is all the more impressive because it specifies that all people will be affected. The mission of Christ is even to include the Gentiles. Still more amazingly, Simeon added that a sword would in time pierce through the soul of Mary, a reference apparently to the cross.

Interpretations of the Cross by Christ

Jesus evidently on many occasions spoke of his death (Matt. 12:40; 16:21; 17:22; 20:17-19; Mark 8:31; 9:31; 10:33-34; and many others). He not only foretold the necessity of it but also indicated its purpose. We read: "Even as the Son of man came not to be ministered unto, but to minister, and to give his life a ramsom for many" (Matt. 20:28). Jesus referred to himself as the "good shepherd" who "giveth his life for the sheep" (John 10:2). He also spoke of the "other sheep" which he possessed and which he would ultimately bring into his fold. His death is here obviously shown to be redemptive in purpose, and for all who would accept its benefits.

Luke quoted Christ as saying regarding his last journey up to Jerusalem that what was about to happen was in accordance with that which had been written in the prophets.

In relating the parable of the wicked husbandmen who slew, not only the servants whom the Lord sent, but also the owner's son, Jesus pointed to himself as the Son. Then he declared: "Whosoever shall fall on this stone [referring to himself] shall be broken: but on whomsoever it shall fall, it will grind him to powder" (Matt. 21:44). Christ is the hope or the judge of all, for the "whosoever" here emphasized includes all men.

A passage of great depth (John 6) records Jesus' teaching about the meaning of his death by use of the symbolism of his own flesh and blood. John quoted Jesus as saying: "Verily, verily I say unto you, Except ye eat the flesh of the Son of man, and drink his blood, ye have no life in you" (John 6:53). Jesus was speaking, not of the literal eating of his flesh or drinking of his blood, but of the spiritual transformation resulting from trusting in him. A similar idea is apparent in Jesus' remark to Nicodemus: "And as Moses lifted up the serpent in the wilderness, even so must the Son of man be lifted up: That whosoever believeth in him should not perish, but have eternal life" (John 3:14-15). John later recorded Jesus as saying: "Except a corn of wheat fall into the ground and die, it abideth alone: but if it die, it bringeth forth much fruit. And I, if I be lifted up from the earth, will draw all men unto me" (John 12:24,32). Jesus was referring in these expressions specifically to his death. In each instance the whole world is included.

We should never overlook the truth, that in his interpretation of his own mission, and especially of his death, Jesus seemed always to have all men in view.

Proclamation of the Cross by the New Testament Church

Many passages throughout the New Testament from Acts to Revelation refer to the death of Christ. They are so numerous that no one can fail to see what the early church understood about the meaning of the cross. Peter and his fellow disciples, for example, preached at Pentecost that the One whom the people had crucified, God had raised up. They then declared: "Let all the house of Israel know assuredly, that God hath made that same Jesus, whom ye have crucified, both Lord and Christ" (Acts 2:36). Christ of the cross is Lord of all.

Paul, the great theologian, later wrote: "For all have sinned, and come short of the glory of God; being justified freely by his grace through the redemption that is in Christ Jesus: whom God hath set forth to be a propitiation through faith in his blood, to declare his righteousness for the remission of sins that are past, through the forbearance of God" (Rom. 3:23-25). All men are here declared guilty of sin. But in the redemption of Christ all men may also have hope. "But God commendeth his love toward us, in that, while we were yet sinners, Christ died for us" (Rom. 5:8). This note is sounded consistently throughout the remainder of the New Testament.

Professor Bengt Sundkler of Upsala College, after having described the reason for the call and training of Israel, says: "So we see that there are two aspects of the universality of the Old Testament: one is in the line of election and blessing [the calling out of Israel] and stretches from Abraham to the Messiah; the other is the line of the Gentiles. The Christian faith claims that they met at the cross." The Old Testament and the New Testament do meet at the cross, as do all nations and all men. The simple statement, "And . . . died for all" (2 Cor. 5:15), is therefore the hope of the world and also a fathomless motive for the world missions enterprise. That death on the cross is truly the instrument for the healing of the nations, and there is no other such instrument.

In conclusion, it may be said the meaning of the cross for world missions includes at least the following:

In the cross Christ judged all men. It was the sins of all men which made his cross necessary.

In the cross Christ disclosed the nature of sin.

In the cross Christ made known the utter helplessness and hopelessness of man to save himself.

In the cross Christ bared the heart of God for all men to see. Never again could any man anywhere rightly doubt the love and mercy of God. That love is so great and that mercy so vast that even the worst and the most unworthy are included.

In the cross Christ provided an adequate remedy for the sins of all men. "But we see Jesus, who was made a little lower than the angels for the suffering of death, crowned with glory and honour; that he by the grace of God should taste death for every man" (Heb. 2:9).

11 —Missions and the Power of the Resurrection

See selected passages in text.

"The young people of today," says President Pusey of Harvard, "are searching for a creed to believe, a song to sing, a flag to follow." So, it seems, is the rest of the world. But Jesus' disciples needed no such search. The resurrection, for example, was not a creed they found but a reality that overtook them. They did not merely believe in the resurrection; they were caught up and transformed by it. It was a discovery, not a conclusion reached by reasoning. Literally overcome with despair by the crucifixion (Luke 24:21), the disciples were so unprepared for the resurrection that their minds at first stubbornly rejected it. Only by force of evidence were they convinced. It would have seemed ridiculous to them then to have been asked, "Do you believe in the resurrection?" They knew it to be a fact.

Too often Christians of today speak of the resurrection as something to believe rather than an incomparable reality to proclaim. The resurrection of Christ remains the great unshakable reality of the ages. From the day of Pentecost the tongues of the disciples, so paralyzed with fear by the cross, never ceased to preach the certainty and the meaning of the resurrection. They saw this event, moreover, as being significant for all the world and for all time. But what is its significance? To fail to examine this ques-is to neglect a keystone in the foundation on which the whole structure of world missions rests.

We live in a day of growing nationalism and of the resurgence of many religions. Missionary activity is becoming a two-way street. For the first time in American history, we are beginning to see missionary movements of other religions invading the so-called Christian West. It becomes urgent, therefore, that the distinctive character of the Christian faith be set forth. This is uniquely done by the truth of the resurrection. This truth declares:

Christ is what he claimed to be. In Romans it is said of Christ that he was "declared to be the Son of God with power, according to the spirit of holiness, by the resurrection from the dead" (Rom. 1:4). Literally, he was openly designated and revealed truly to be the Son of God in power by his resurrection. This is the infallible proof that he is God the Son, that he is all he ever affirmed himself to be. If this be so—and we can only accept it or reject it as we must accept or reject any other historic fact—then no other religion offers a Saviour like Christ or knows anyone comparable to him. The resurrection is undeniable proof that God has broken through to us in the person of Christ and actually, as Jesus so often said, has truly revealed himself in Christ to our wondering eyes.

What Christ taught is not only true but is also of crucial, enduring, and inescapable significance. If men live face to face with the risen Son of God, then what he says takes on significance far greater than anything else ever uttered. It is little wonder, therefore, that we are reminded in Hebrews: "God, who at sundry times and in divers manners spake in time past unto the fathers by the prophets, hath in these last days spoken unto us by his Son . . . Therefore we ought to give the more earnest heed to the things which we have heard" (Heb. 1:1-2; 2:1). If Christ had not risen, then men could well ignore what he said; but in the light of the resurrection, eternal consequences hang on their acceptance or rejection of what Jesus said. He himself remarked: "Verily, verily, I say unto you, He that heareth my word, and believeth on him that sent me, hath everlasting life, and shall not come into condemnation; but is passed from death unto life" (John 5:24). He said, moreover: "Heaven and earth shall pass away, but my words shall not pass away" (Matt. 24:35). Even more pointedly he remarked: "He that rejecteth me, and receiveth not my words, hath one that judgeth him: the word that I have spoken, the same shall judge him in the last day" (John 12:48). Every man's destiny is determined by whether he accepts or rejects Jesus' word. If, as the writer of Hebrews impressively observed, God who once spoke through chosen men now is speaking to us through his very Son, how indeed shall men escape if they neglect the salvation he offers?

God's redemptive grace and purpose truly embrace all men. This is a precious assurance.

The sins of all the world had made the cross necessary. If, as the resurrection attests, Christ was not a mere man, but the Son of God, his resurrection affects not the Jews alone but all men. No wonder Christ gave directions to his disciples after his resurrection that their witness was to embrace the whole earth—Jerusalem, Judea, Samaria, and the "uttermost part" (Acts 1:8). When seen from this view, it is obvious that all Jesus had done, now climaxed by his resurrection, was a part of God's long declared redemptive plan and can be explained only by God's grace (Rom. 5:15). To men everywhere the cross reveals the glory and greatness of God's love, and the resurrection forever affirms it. God who loved the world enough to give his Son to die for it still loves it enough to want to save it (Rom. 4:25).

The final and most fearful foes of mankind have been forever overcome. Man's needs and enemies may vary from place to place. The incidence, for example, of disease or the degree of suffering or the blight of ignorance may vary. The two common, inescapable, and final foes of all the race, however, are death and the grave. Despite medical science and increased knowledge, these foes strike people alike in all parts of the world. Nor does anyone in his wildest imagination conceive of a time when these foes can actually be eliminated. In no way known to man, save in Christ, has victory over death and the grave ever been assured. But Jesus promised: "He that believeth in me, though he were dead, yet shall he live: and whosoever liveth and believeth in me shall never die" (John 11:25-26). Paul could also joyously declare: "He that raised up Christ from the dead shall also quicken your mortal bodies by his Spirit" (Rom. 8:11). Through the triumph of the resurrection, death for the enlightened Christian anywhere in the world loses its dread and becomes only a servant by which a soul is led into fuller life beyond. Truly, "Jesus Christ . . . hath abolished death, and hath brought life and immortality to light" (2 Tim. 1:10). One of the saddest spectacles in the earth and that which most typifies the hopelessness and emptiness of men outside of Christ everywhere is how they look upon death. Yet what Christ has done for man in conquering death and the grave is a glorious benefit available to every soul everywhere.

Spiritual resurrection is possible for every man. Not only does the resurrection assure believers universally of victory over the grave and death, it also provides them assurance of their own spiritual resurrection now. Paul had this in mind apparently when he wrote: "Therefore we are buried with him by baptism into death: that like as Christ was raised up from the dead by the glory of the Father, even so we also should walk in newness of life. If we have been planted together in the likeness of his death, we shall be also in the likeness of his resurrection: knowing this, that our old man is crucified with him, that the body of sin might be destroyed, that henceforth we should not serve sin. . . . Now if we be dead with Christ, we believe that we shall also live with him" (Rom. 6:4-8). The Scriptures reveal that the sinner is spiritually dead. Unreconciled to God through Christ and existing in a state of disobedience, he is "dead in trespasses and sins" (Eph. 2:1). Through Christ those who are spiritually dead can be made alive or "quickened." Thus we read: "But God, who is rich in mercy, for his great love wherewith he loved us, even when we were dead in sins, hath quickened us together with Christ (by grace ye are saved); and hath raised us up together, and made us sit together in heavenly places in Christ Jesus" (Eph. 2:4-6). The believer anywhere in the world is enabled to rejoice with Peter: "Blessed be the God and Father of our Lord Jesus Christ, which according to his abundant mercy hath begotten us again unto a lively hope [living hope] by the resurrection of Jesus Christ from the dead" (1 Peter 1:3).

The mission given the church has the authority of the living God as its source and its necessity. How great is the responsibility of those who have found Christ to carry out his mission! That mission is not optional. Christians have no right to choose whether they will engage in missionary enterprises. The urgent nature of our task arises out of the lordship and authority of the risen Christ. Jesus declared after the resurrection: "All power [authority] is given unto me in heaven and in earth. Go ye, therefore, and teach all nations, baptizing them in the name of the Father, and of the Son, and of the Holy Ghost: Teaching them to observe all things whatsoever I have commanded you: and, lo, I am with you alway, even unto the end of the world" (Mat. 28:18-20). If the supreme Lord of the universe, as the resurrection proves Christ to be, demands it, how can any one of us oppose it?

Every soul exists beyond death. At least one other profoundly important lesson for missions is amply revealed by the resurrection. If Jesus made any one fact clear, it is that the soul of man has a destiny beyond the grave. He spoke of certain personalities of the past as still living. In the transfiguration he met with Moses and Elijah. He himself raised the son of a widow at Nain and Lazarus also from the dead. He spoke specifically of the judgment scene to which all nations will be gathered and of the separation to be made among men to their eternal destiny (Matt. 25). Paul wrote of the resurrection "of the just and unjust" (Acts 24:15). He said also: "This corruptible must put on incorruption, and this mortal must put on immortality" (1 Cor. 15:53). To the Thessalonians he stated: "But I would not have you to be ignorant, brethren, concerning them which are asleep [deceased], that ye sorrow not, even as others which have no hope. For if we believe that Jesus died and rose again, even so them also which sleep in Jesus will God bring with him" (1 Thess. 4:13-14). John in Revelation revealed: "And I saw the dead, small and great, stand before God; and the books were opened: and another book was opened, which is the book of life; and the dead were judged out of those things which were written in the books, according to their works" (Rev. 20:12). Paul preached that man's last enemy, death, shall be destroyed (1 Cor. 15:26). This is assurance for every Christian.

Without the resurrection men might well believe, as atheists and Communists argue, that there is nothing beyond the grave. The resurrection, however, makes this impossible. It also reveals that the most important dimension of life is one's relationship to Christ. For in that relationship eternal destiny is determined.

If Christians could capture or recapture the vivid, burning certainty the early church possessed concerning the resurrection, they would surely need no further motivation for a missionary advance great enough literally to take the world for Christ. In the burning and profoundly convincing certainty that Christ was alive from the dead and thus an ever-present and universally reigning Lord and merciful Saviour, the early church conquered a hostile and pagan world and turned it to him. Similarly moved, the Christian hosts of our day could do it again.

12—Missions in the Commissions

Matthew 28:18-20; Mark 13:10; 16:15-16; Luke 24:46-49; John 20:21-23; Acts 1:8

Christianity is a world religion. It has been a missionary religion from the beginning. The commissions of Christ to his disciples disclose without doubt that Jesus so intended it to be. This chapter will examine his commissions to see what missionary obligations they especially place upon the followers of Christ. We are accustomed to thinking only of the Great Commission given in Matthew, but actually Jesus appears to have given several commissions. Let us now look at these commissions.

The Great Commission

The first, the so-called Great Commission just mentioned (Matt. 28:18-20), literally stated is: "All authority in heaven and on earth is given me. Having gone, therefore, disciple ye all the nations, baptizing them into the name of the Father and of the Son and of the Holy Spirit, keeping on teaching them to observe all things whatever I gave command to you." The main verb in this commission is *make*, not *go*. The verb *go* is a participle in the Greek. To make disciples is to evangelize or to lead men to the acceptance of Christ as Lord and Saviour and thus to an experience of the new birth. To become a disciple is to be his follower and constant learner.

Christ's Commission in Mark

A second commission of our Lord, found in Mark 16:15-16, again literally stated is: "And he said unto them; having gone into the world, all of it, proclaim ye (or herald) the gospel to all the creation. The one believing and being baptized will be saved, but the one disbelieving will be condemned." The phrase "believe and be baptized" is clarified by verse 16. Believing is the decisive first step in one's response. It is only for disbelieving, not for failing to be baptized, that one will be condemned. Again Jesus did not put the emphasis on going but rather upon proclaiming the gospel. The word translated go here means having gone. The objective is proclaiming the gospel to all the creation, or all created beings.

The task of the church is not, therefore, merely geographical—that is, getting the gospel to every continent and nation—but personal and universal. No person in all creation is to be left out.

Christ's Commission in Luke

A third commission is found in Luke 24:46-49: "And he said unto them, Thus it is written, and thus it behoved Christ to suffer, and to rise from the dead the third day: and that repentance and remission of sins should be preached in his name among all nations, beginning at Jerusalem. And ye are witnesses of these things. And, behold, I send the promise of my Father upon you: but tarry ye in the city of Jerusalem, until ye be endued with power from on high." Repentance is to lead to the remission or forgiveness of sins. And proclamation is to be made in the name of Christ, beginning from Jerusalem and extending into all the nations.

Christ's Commission in John

A fourth commission appears in John 20:21-23: "Then said Jesus to them again, Peace be unto you: as my Father hath sent me, even so send I you. And when he had said this, he breathed on them, and saith unto them, Receive ye the Holy Ghost: Whose soever sins ye remit, they are remitted unto them; and whose soever sins ye retain, they are retained." The puzzling promise given in verse 23 should be interpreted by references to Matthew 16:19; 18:19. The point seems to be that by proclamation of the gospel men are brought to the knowledge of Christ. If Christians fail in this task, then men will be left in their state of lostness and unforgiveness and thus bound forever. If this interpretation is accurate, and it is supported by some able students, then obviously it suggests an awesome responsibility.

Christ's Commission in Acts

The fifth commission is found in Acts 1:8: "But ye shall receive power, after that the Holy Ghost is come upon you: and ye shall be witnesses unto me both in Jerusalem, and in all Judea, and in Samaria, and unto the uttermost part of the earth."

Summary of Christ's Commissions

Putting together all these various expressions of the commissions of our Lord we are led to certain specific conclusions concerning the missionary enterprise and the world task of Christians for all ages. Some of these are summarized in the following paragraphs.

The commissions are made authoritative by the Lordship of the risen Christ. Having triumphed over the grave and death, Jesus asserted that "all authority" had been given to him. On the basis of this authority and of his kingship, he stated his orders to his followers. Jesus had fulfilled the Old Testament prophecies concerning his messiahship and kingship. As the risen Lord, he gave expression to his universal message and issued his universal commands. Identifying himself evidently as the Son of man mentioned in Daniel 7:13 and the suffering Servant of Isaiah 53, Christ proclaimed his worldwide Commission on the basis of his absolute and universal authority.

The commissions indicate that the field of missions extends from one's own local center—wherever that is—to the world's perimeter. For the disciples that center was Jerusalem, but this was to be a place of beginning, "beginning at Jerusalem" (Luke 24:47). In his final commission Jesus made this emphasis even clearer by specifying Judea, Samaria, and the uttermost part of the earth (Acts 1:8). Christianity is a world religion, including local as well as world needs. No one is to overlook his responsibility to be a missionary at home. Unless missions begins here, it has no meaning there. It is a grave inconsistency either to be concerned about foreign missions when we have no interest in home missions, or in home missions when we have no burden for foreign missions.

The commissions disclose that the primary means of carrying out world missions is by witnessing. A witness is one who bears testimony as to what he knows and bears it in any place of need. One who has met Christ and come to know him truly has something about which to witness. His responsibility to bear this witness is not optional. Jesus said to his disciples, "Ye shall be witnesses" (Acts 1:8). The truth is that no Christian has a right to choose to be or not to be a witness. Automatically, by virtue of his profession of faith, he immediately is made a witness. His witness may be positive or negative, good or bad, but he is still a witness. If his witness is unworthy, then it denies the Christ he professes. All we are and say and do, of course, combine to make our witness. One's chief witness is in a changed life manifested before the world.

A second witness comes through acts of service to others in the name of Christ.

A third witness, and this becomes all the more effective when it is based on the first two, is in word. Wherever we are and whenever the opportunity allows, we are expected to bear witness by word of mouth, but always in every circumstance—at work, in travel, at home, in school—Christians are witnesses for or against Christ. This, all the commissions seem clearly to testify.

The commissions disclose that every Christian is responsible in some way for the world task of missions. Our chief responsibility is to make disciples. The Lord calls some, as he did Paul, to go to distant lands; but he calls all of us to be makers of disciples, no matter where we are. Those whom he calls for service beyond their home environs have no alternative, if obedient, but to go. The rest of us have a responsibility, of course, to help enable these who are so called to go. But how urgent it is that everyone who professes Christ also understand that he is already somewhere and wherever he is, he is to help disciple all nations.

The commissions assure us that the strength needed for the world task of missions will be provided. The presence of the Holy Spirit and his unfailing strength are always available. "Behold, I send the promise of my Father upon you," said Christ (Luke 24:49). Were it not for this assurance our task would seem overwhelming and impossible. Confronted with the present awesome needs of men, Christians in this day cannot help trembling over the magnitude of their task. But they are not required to go in their own strength, nor do they depend on their own wisdom alone. The Holy Spirit is always with them.

The commissions reveal that the basic objective of the global missionary enterprise is changed men. "As my Father hath sent me," Jesus declared, "even so send I you" (John 20:21). He had said earlier of himself, "The Son of man is come to seek and to save that which was lost" (Luke 19:10). This is the glorious and inescapable objective of all missionary endeavor.

The commissions imply that no man can ever have any ground of hope (or of life) outside Christ. "He that believeth . . . shall be saved, but he that believeth not shall be damned" (Mark 16:16). If Christ ever made one thing clear, it is that there is no other way to the Father but by him. He who does not believe on him will be forever lost (John 3:16-18). The world compass of the Master's commissions reveals that all men were included in this judgment. There is simply no hope of a right relationship with God or of life itself except as one finds and believes on the Lord Jesus Christ.

The commissions reveal that the method of changing men is through the preaching of repentance which leads to the remission of sins (Luke 24:47). In bearing witness to Christ and making known the grace of God, Christians must ever emphasize the needs of natural man; namely, his sinfulness and lostness, his estrangement from God, and his condemnation in sin. The only way out of this condition is through repentance, the turning about of the whole life, the change of the heart and of the mind toward God, the turning from a course of evil and rebellion to obedience and faith. Such repentance leads to the remission or forgiveness of sins and to the removal of guilt. "He that believeth on him shall be saved" (Mark 16:16).

The commissions make clear that, though changed men is the ultimate goal of all missionary endeavor, the task of missions does not end here. The Great Commission calls for the unceasing work of teaching the evangelized and helping them to grow toward Christian maturity. The main task, as already noted, is to make disciples; but those won are then to be unceasingly taught the commands of Christ that they may become full-grown Christians. Jesus' promise, "Lo, I am with you alway" (Matt. 28:20) follows, and seems based upon the fulfilment of this command. No new Christian is ever born full-grown spiritually as no child is born full-grown physically. One of the gravest responsibilities resting upon the church in its ministry both at home and abroad is to help those who become Christians to grow toward Christian adulthood.

13—Power Given for World Witness

Acts 1 and 2

The sheer magnitude of the global scope of missions would make the task seem impossible of fulfilment but for one fact. Over half the world has never heard of Christ, and another fourth of its people have no true conception of his meaning. How can the church cope with such a task?

Many proposals could perhaps be offered. There is only one basic answer. In the previous chapter the various commissions of our Lord were examined. The commission found in Acts 1:8 reveals the power available for the task. Jesus had told the disciples that they would be "baptized with the Holy Ghost not many days hence" (Acts 1:5). They then asked: "Lord, wilt thou at this time restore again the kingdom to Israel?" (Acts 1:6). Some have been perplexed by this question, concluding that the disciples were still under the old Hebrew impression that the kingdom of David would be restored in a natural sense. They wanted to know when this would occur.

If this view were correct, how could Peter and the other disciples have been so sure ten days hence as to the purpose of Christ and their own mission in relationship to it? It seems wiser to understand their question to mean, "Lord, when will you bring to consummation (or completion) the kingdom you have come to establish?"

The Missions Task Is Awesome

But how could such a task be completed? If the church's mission today seems awesome, how much more so it must have appeared to the first disciples. Only a few in number, they faced a whole world, hostile and committed to paganism. We, like the early disciples, must be assisted by a power beyond our own. Fortunately, that power is available.

It is the power provided in the person of the Holy Spirit. "But ye shall receive power, after that the Holy Ghost is come upon you: and ye shall be witnesses unto me both in Jerusalem, and in all Judea, and in Samaria, and unto the uttermost part of the earth" (Acts 1:8). Ability, efficiency, and might! These are his gifts which make the difference.

The Holy Spirit Guides and Directs

This promise of the Master was not limited merely to the disciples of that day or only to those who heard Peter (Acts 2:38-39) but was universal and unceasing. Peter proclaimed: "For the promise is unto you, and to your children, and to all that are afar off, even as many as the Lord our God shall call" (Acts 2:39). This promise, therefore, clearly includes all succeeding generations. But what special help does the Holy Spirit provide, and in what way is the power promised through him to be expressed?

A negative answer ought first to be given. It is that this power is not to be a substitute for any other gift God bestows upon us. The help the Holy Spirit provides, for example, does not relieve the church of the need of organization or promotion in its missionary or other services. Nor does the power afforded relieve Christians either of the need of intelligence or the preparation of their minds for service. The Spirit will help us learn more and more about the Bible and how to use available constructive methods and means available to us. It is our responsibility to search for and intelligently make the wisest use of what he provides, remembering always that he alone can make anything we possess or do useful and fruitful.

The Spirit may and often fortunately does use persons of limited education and native ability for an effective witness in the name of Christ. This fact does not relieve anyone of his obligation to prepare himself in every possible way for larger usefulness. The missionary, for example, though he may be confident of the Spirit's presence with him wherever he goes, is not to serve among another people until he knows that people, their language, and the means by which they can best be reached. This requires long study and preparation.

The Holy Spirit Strengthens Christians

Now looking at the positive answer as to how the Holy Spirit strengthens Christians for world-encompassing missionary service, at least five facts ought to be noted and these are drawn from the experience of the early disciples:

He provides convincing understanding of the meaning, purpose, and transforming power of Christ. We have seen in a previous study of the work of the Holy Spirit that one of his ministries would be to call to mind the things Christ had taught and also to be a teacher himself of these things (John 14-16). Thus the message proclaimed by the early disciples was given unique authority. The disciples truly became trustworthy interpreters and authentic witnesses. Multitudes who first heard them became convinced of this and thus were brought under conviction by what they heard.

He gives "tongues" to the timid and courage to the cowering. It will not be forgotten that, at the arrest of Christ, sheer terror and dismay laid hold of his disciples and their tongues were tied by it. Obviously, it must have been something of great significance which had occurred to the disciples that enabled them no longer to fear any man. Their tongues gloriously loosed, they declared the truth about Jesus everywhere. Any person who allows the Spirit to use him and to use all the resources God has given him can overcome fear and timidity, and can be used beyond comprehension as a witness.

He overcomes barriers of communication. One of the most notable effects of the coming of the Holy Spirit upon the early disciples was the remarkable capacity given them to speak in languages understood by all the great variety of national and linguistic representatives in the city at the time. Those who heard were no less astounded than the disciples at this phenomenon. They asked, "And how hear we every man in our own tongue, wherein we were born?" (Acts 2:8). Overcome by such a miraculous development, it seemed obvious to them that something beyond human ability had been given to the disciples.

Though the Spirit may not continue in quite the same way to give power of communication to Christians, he does continue to aid them in the mastery of the languages of various peoples of the world and to build bridges of communication to them. Portions of the Scriptures have been translated already into more than 1,250 languages. The Holy Spirit waits even now, we must believe, to help Christians make the gospel available in the more than two thousand languages into which it has not yet been translated. He seeks, moreover, the response of individual Christians to the ever-present challenge to overcome every barrier of communication which may prevent getting the gospel to every creature on the earth.

He makes persuasive the witness borne. Jesus had said, "Ye shall be [my] witnesses" (Acts 1:8). It is obvious from the context that the disciples did become witnesses. It should be obvious also that no Christian is justified in excusing himself from bearing witness, either in spoken or written word, as well as in life. In classroom, in shop, in business office, on airplanes or trains, in taxis, in homes, and in hundreds of other places there are daily opportunities for such witnessing. The pity and the tragedy are that these opportunities are so often forgotten or forfeited.

It is obvious that early disciples bore witness, not only by what they said, but also in the quality of life they manifested. One thing which made their preaching convincing to all who heard them was that something had made a difference in them (Acts 2:47).

It has been wisely said that every person is either missionary or a missions field. A Christian automatically becomes a missionary by his profession of Christ as Lord and Saviour. His witness should be borne thereafter both in word and in life. When these are properly combined, the Holy Spirit is prepared to own and bless that witness and to make it bear fruit. As the field of the world is now and evermore "white already to harvest" (John 4:35), the followers of the Lord Jesus Christ may be assured that adequate power is constantly available to them through the Holy Spirit to make them equal to their task and ever gloriously fruitful.

He awakens conviction in the hearts of the hearers. "They were pricked in their heart, and said . . . Men and brethren, what shall we do?" (Acts 2:37). That was the response at Pentecost to the preaching of the disciples who had truly given themselves to the mastery and use of the Holy Spirit!

It is not within our human power to bring conviction of the guilt of sin and a sense of the necessity of a change to other lives apart from the work of the Spirit. Indeed, the Holy Spirit alone can accomplish that mysterious and marvelous work. He will do it, apparently, as Christians meet the conditions the early Christians so well met; namely, waiting until they were endued with his power.

That waiting, however, was not a passive idleness or a mere marking of time, but a period engaged in prayer, fellowship, faith, and full surrender to the Lord, to whom they had given their lives. This apparently is the universal condition upon which the Holy Spirit can be expected to anoint and use Christians.

14—Witness Which Began to Get the World in View

Acts 3 to 7

The Power of the Christian Message

In a call directed to today's complacent and comfort-loving church, Paul Stevens of the Radio and Television Commission says the modern Christian can hardly imagine the power with which the Christian message burst upon the world in its beginning. He declares, moreover, that Christianity is even now "the ultimate weapon." No other "weapon" has promise, he insists, of overcoming the evil of communism or of human degeneracy in general. In truth, the changing of our tension-laden world for good awaits the work of Christianity.

But that Christianity which proves to be the ultimate weapon cannot be self-centered. It cannot merely seek its own security and exhaust its resources on building bigger buildings, programs, and budgets. A resurgence of New Testament Christianity is required if it is to be effective.

Dr. Kenneth Chafin ventures the opinion that when Jesus gave the disciples the commission, as stated in Acts 1:8, what the disciples actually thought they heard was: "You shall be my witnesses unto the *Jews* who are in Jerusalem and to the *Jews* in all Judea, and Samaria and to the ends of the earth." To some degree this judgment appears undeniable. Yet there are encouraging evidences that, even from Christ's ascension, the disciples began truly to get the whole world in view. This accomplishment was not easy for them, as it is not for us. Quite a struggle must have gone on for some time before they saw the truth. Some in the early church may never have gotten their eyes open. Indeed it is probable as we shall later see that the Jerusalem church for this very reason lost its golden opportunity to be the first to send out missionaries to the rest of the world even though it was the first Christian congregation on earth. It forgot, or failed quite to understand, that Christ had charged it to keep the whole world in its view.

Fortunately, however, there were some things the disciples remembered from the three-year "graduate" course given them by Christ before his crucifixion. In time the Holy Spirit was to bring to their memory many other things he had also tried to teach them.

Enlarged Horizons After Pentecost

A careful reading of Acts 3 to 7 gives evidence that from the day of Pentecost enlarged horizons of responsibility began soon to be seen by growing numbers in the church. Acts 3 begins by noting Peter's and John's going up to the Temple at the hour of prayer (around midafternoon) and seeing as they went a certain man, crippled from his birth, being carried to the gate of the Temple called Beautiful where he could beg for charitable gifts. How many years this had been a daily experience for him we are not told. We are informed that Peter and John were arrested themselves by the sight of this cripple. Here was a representative of the world of the afflicted, a world which lay all about them, but one which they perhaps had hardly been able to see until they saw it through the eyes of Jesus.

A great evangelistic witness had been made at Pentecost, and was still being made. Thousands had been led to believe in Christ and join the church. But in the midst of all of this there was also evidenced a concern to help the physically handicapped and suffering. This poor crippled man, dependent likely on some relatives or on anyone he could persuade to help him, had no hope of healing but only of existing. This changed when Peter and John stopped that day. Expecting at best perhaps only a coin in his cup, he discovered through Peter and John a greater source of assistance than this. "Silver and gold have I none," said Peter, "but such as I have give I thee" (Acts 3:6). Then in the name of Jesus Christ of Nazareth, Peter commanded the man to rise and walk!

Is it not still in the power of the church, when possessed with sufficient desire, to minister healingly to the helpless, hopeless, afflicted, and needy beyond anything presently imagined? How hard it is even today for us to get this part of the world clearly enough in view to be concerned for its need.

The world even now, despite the amazing medical and scientific developments of recent times, is almost a sea of affliction and suffering. What if it knew that there were people who really loved them for Christ's sake and truly cared? Let God be praised for the service of a host of life-committed missionary doctors and nurses and also for an increasing number of other workers committed to help the masses around the world. But how many others like them are needed.

A World in Spiritual Bondage

The early disciples saw more, however, than the world of physical need. They also saw a world in spiritual bondage. They began to sense what later they were to see far more clearly, that the hope of every man in the world depends on his personal relationship to Christ. In explaining to the astonished multitudes who beheld the lame man now cured as to how this marvel came about, Peter and John reminded their hearers that the One whom they had denied is the Holy One and the Just, and that in crucifying him they had "killed the Prince of life" (Acts 3:14-15).

The Christ whom they had denied, rejected, and killed, these apostles said, in truth was the same Source and Author of life. Possibly the disciples then were primarily interested only in their fellow Jews. But they did see them as lost and without hope except as they came to this Christ whom God had raised from the dead. Referring to the Old Testament prophecies, and especially to what Moses had said, they declared: "It shall come to pass, that every soul, which will not hear that prophet [Jesus, the Messiah], shall be destroyed from among the people" (Acts 3:23). This was to say that the mere fact that Jews were descendants of Abraham gave them no hope. They, too, must "hear" Christ.

Though the disciples may not, as yet, have quite caught the full vision of the magnitude of the lostness of all men outside Christ, they at least saw that their own nation had no hope apart from his redemptive work. In stressing the lostness of every soul, however, they must have seen that all other men were lost, too, without this Christ; that there was no hope for anyone, Jew or Gentile, outside him.

God Concerned for All Men

The disciples began to see even more. They discovered what they would later fully and clearly see—that the world purpose and plan of God concerned the whole human race. When called before the rulers of the Jews to explain what they had done for the "impotent man" (Acts 4:9), they testified with courage that is astounding and with self-forgetfulness and apparent willingness to risk life itself: "This [Christ] is the stone which was set at nought of you builders, which is become the head of the corner" (Acts 4:11). More boldly, they added with burning conviction the universal judgment: "Neither is there salvation in any other: for there is none other name under heaven given among men, whereby we must be saved" (Acts 4:12). They were dogmatic in their claims concerning Christ.

We shall later see, to be sure, that it was difficult for the disciples to apply their own preaching when the personal tests came. But at least they now apparently understood Christ to be the only hope of men everywhere. They had discovered by such convincing evidence that it wholly possessed and controlled them, that in the risen Christ alone—the One pure and holy, just and blameless, and the very source of life itself—could one ever find life or eternal hope.

They had found, too, that the only way to find life in Christ was to repent and be converted; that is, to turn completely around (Acts 3:19). Thus they promised, "Your sins may be blotted out." Such a turning to Christ would result, moreover, they preached, in a refreshing and an "epoch-making" period of spiritual revival in the very presence of the Lord. For the Jews this would mean that they would come to know the long-awaited Messiah and in him discover a Saviour.

Early Church With a World View

Finally, the early church bore a witness which began truly to get the whole world in view because it also discovered the breadth and meaning of the sovereignty of God.

The authorities of the Jews had failed utterly to stop the disciples from witnessing (preaching) concerning the saving power of Christ *(see Acts 4:10-12).* These rulers called the disciples before their court and demanded that they cease to teach in or even to mention the name of Jesus. One of the high moments in the history of the early church came in this very hour when the disciples, through Peter and John replied, "Whether it be right in the sight of God to hearken unto you more than unto God, judge ye. For we cannot but speak the things which we have seen and heard" (Acts 4:19-20).

These followers of Christ had come to an experience and a discovery which made them absolute debtors and compelled them to bear their witness to all. They had found, moreover, that to accept Christ as Saviour required them also to confess him as Lord. This meant also that they had to accept the universal sovereignty of God. To obey him would hereafter be their only motive, to fail him their only fear. If his plan encompassed the whole earth, their program could include no less. If men objected to their message or forbade their witness, they had no option but to obey God.

One of the most outstanding sermons ever recorded was the message which Stephen preached as recorded in Acts 7:2-53. It charged Stephen's fellow Jews with having resisted and failed God at every crucial point of their history and came to a climax with further charge that they had slain the "Just One," of whom in their act they had been the betrayers! This powerful message was evidently but a sample of the driving force of the conviction and sense of duty early Christians felt. Their position as witnesses of Christ, under the sovereignty and plan of God, had laid a duty upon them they could not avoid, even if the cost was death. Fulfilment of Christian responsibility of this order could lead again, as with Stephen, to beholding of "the glory of God" (Acts 7:55).

Stephen, who has been appropriately called that "God-crowned, sunlit layman," bore a witness none could ever forget. Not ever, as we shall later see, was Saul of Tarsus, who voted for his death and was zealous to blot out the name of the Christ whom Stephen proclaimed, able to forget him. It is a strong possibility, as many suspect, that the haunting memory of Stephen's message and martyrdom for Christ that day had a remarkable bearing upon preparing Saul for the revelation he received later on the Damascus Road.

Stephen took the lordship of Christ over his life seriously. What a contrast this is with most of us modern Christians. Early Christians, captivated by the call to world witness, feared not even the loss of life for that witness.

15—Witness Which Won Jew and Gentile

Acts 8 to 12

Both Jew and Gentile are found in the events related to the birth of Christ: "Now when Jesus was born in Bethlehem of Judea in the days of Herod the king, behold, there came wise men from the east to Jerusalem, saying, Where is he that is born King of the Jews? for we have seen his star in the east and are come to worship him" (Matt. 2:1-2). This reference tends to show that Jesus was the Messiah, and to honor him in bringing out the respect paid him by distinguished Gentiles.

Jews had difficulty, however, in accepting this idea. Despite all the prophets had said, they persisted in the belief that somehow they had a special standing with God. That they had been chosen, not as a special favor, but as a channel of blessing to all nations was difficult to conceive. It is striking, therefore, to find in the early verses of Matthew's Gospel an account of the coming of Gentiles bringing gifts to and worshiping at the feet of the newborn Babe.

The incident suggests that Gentiles as well as Jews were in God's gracious plan of redemption. Yet it was not easy even for the disciples at first to accept the truth that all men, regardless of race, national background, social status, or religious belief, should receive the gospel.

The task of world missions was perhaps at first considered by believers to be primarily geographical; that is, to Jerusalem, Judea, and Samaria, and thereafter to the distant parts of the earth. Yet the early church did see its mission as more than geographical. It was devoutly concerned to help all believers understand that commitment to Christ as Lord and Saviour required men to help to redeem and change every area of life and relationship about them. It is possible that present-day Christians fail to comprehend, as well as did the early disciples, those full demands of our faith.

The frontiers of missions today may have changed somewhat. They may include the cities with their teeming millions, the academic realm, where life-changing ideas are fashioned, or the realm of social tensions which seem to grow ever more serious. Yet there are also vast geographical areas which are still wholly untouched by the gospel. More than half the world, we are told, is still in total darkness concerning either Christ's glorious birth at Bethlehem or his triumph at Easter.

The book of Acts affords an exciting account of how early followers of Christ, as they grasped the implications of their world-wide mission, went everywhere preaching the gospel. And hereby hangs a tale of moving power.

Persecution Propels the Gospel Throughout Judea and Samaria

The persecution of the church, which became intense following the death of Stephen, resulted in scattering the church from Jerusalem. These believers did not depart in a spirit of defeat or loss of heart, however, but turned their persecution into an occasion to proclaim the good tidings of Christ all over Judea, and even in Samaria.

In Samaria! Let no one slip past that phrase lightly. It will be difficult to conceive how remarkable was the change which had led these followers of Christ to take the gospel to Samaria. To them, Samaritans were "untouchables," a mixed race of virtual outcasts. Jesus had sought to correct this view by such accounts as that of a man who had fallen among thieves and was rescued by a Samaritan, rather than by a Jewish priest or a Levite. The story must have made many who heard it, including the disciples, flinch with pain. Actually, on one occasion the disciples themselves wanted to call down fire from heaven upon a Samaritan village which had not welcomed Christ. Now, however, they were so concerned to see the Samaritans saved that, in accord with their commission, they readily took the gospel to them. Thus one of the most serious barriers which separates mankind, racial prejudice, was overcome by Christian concern.

Philip, one of the first deacons in the church in Jerusalem, was the first to go to Samaria (Acts 8:5). The response to his ministry was so remarkable that the apostles in Jerusalem sent Peter and John to observe what was taking place in Samaria (Acts 8:14-15). Having satisfied themselves, they later returned to Jerusalem; but on their way, they too "preached the gospel in many villages of the Samaritans" (Acts 8:25).

Early Christians when scattered by persecution sowed the seed of the gospel wherever they went. What if the millions of American Christians annually touring various parts of the world were engaged in similar sowing? A foreign missionary was once heard to say that a great hindrance to the work of the missionary abroad is the un-Christian conduct of so many overseas traveling Americans.

Philip later was led of the Spirit toward Gaza, where he met an African official, evidently a Gentile proselyte to the Jewish faith. The marvelous story of how Philip led this Ethiopian eunuch to belief in Christ is a memorable study in personal soul-winning. The gospel was truly beginning to reach the "uttermost part of the earth" (Acts 1:8).

In almost every city of the United States there are nationals from many countries of the world who could be a far-reaching influence in their world if they were led to Christ.

Paul's Conversion and Appointment as a Missionary to the Gentiles

The young, intellectual Saul of Tarsus, whom we first met as he consented to the stoning of Stephen, was in time to make a complete about-face in his career. On the Damascus road a great light shone about him; and a voice spoke to him, saying: "Saul, Saul, why persecutest thou me?" (Acts 9:4). The story is well-known of how he was led to become a believer himself in Christ and was to be a chosen vessel "to bear [his] name before the Gentiles, and kings, and the children of Israel" (Acts 9:15). Thus one of the most devout and gifted young men of his time was empowered to break out of narrow prejudice and made to see that

Christ died for Jew and Gentile, for every man. After his conversion Paul preached to the Jews in Damascus with telling effect, for it is said: "Saul increased the more in strength and confounded the Jews which dwelt at Damascus, proving that this is the very Christ" (Acts 9:22). For a time also in Jerusalem, he spoke boldly in the name of the Lord Jesus until danger to his life caused the apostles to persuade him to return to Tarsus. Barnabas, who had befriended Paul in Jerusalem, later persuaded him to return to Antioch to assist in the ministry of the gospel in that city (Acts 9:30; 11:25).

Peter Persuaded to Preach to the Gentiles

Peter, while in Joppa, received a vision that was to change his life. In that vision, he was told: "What God hath cleansed, that call not thou common" (Acts 10:15). This led him to a discovery of new horizons. He now understood that afterward his mission as a witness for Christ was to have no boundaries. Not even dislike for Romans was to be an excuse for not responding to the request to him from the Gentile Cornelius. Peter proclaimed the gospel to Cornelius and to all assembled with him. His own words must have sounded strange even to him as they fell from his lips: "Of a truth, I perceive that God is no respecter of persons: but in every nation he that feareth him, and worketh righteousness, is accepted with him" (Acts 10:34-35). He declared, moreover, that to Christ all the prophets gave witness, that through his name "whosoever believeth in him shall receive remission of sins" (Acts 10:43). "Whosoever" includes every man everywhere. Even Peter was astonished at the work of the Holy Spirit in the lives of Cornelius and his household.

There were still those in the church at Jerusalem, however, who did not understand the full meaning of the Great Commission and "contended" with Peter upon his return from his visit with Cornelius. It is to their credit that after Peter and those with him had told what had transpired in Caesarea they apparently were convinced; for it is said: "When they heard these things, they held their peace, and glorified God, saying, Then hath God also to the Gentiles granted repentance unto life" (Acts 11:18).

It was not without a struggle that these early Christians were enabled to embrace the whole world, regardless of race, nation, or other barrier in their concern. That they did so is to their everlasting credit. One may well ask whether we are capable of doing as well.

Persecution continued to scatter Christians, but this only meant the further spreading of the glorious good news they were privileged to bear. Some traveled as far as Phenice, and Cyprus, and Antioch, preaching the word "to none but unto the Jews only" (Acts 11:19). At Antioch they preached also to the Grecians. The gospel here had liberty among both the Jews and Gentiles. "And the hand of the Lord was with them: and a great number believed, and turned unto the Lord" (Acts 11: 21). The news reached Jerusalem, and Barnabas was sent to assist. Finding the work greater than he could do alone, Baranbas went for Saul to help. So marked was the impact of the witness of Christ there and the change in the lives of believers in that city that fellow citizens began to call them "Christians," the noblest term ever used to describe a people. This was the first time Christ's followers were so designated (Acts 11:26).

No one should underrate the problems confronted by the disciples both in the change required in their own thinking and in the forces they met in their conquest for Christ. They encountered closed-mindedness among the Jews, prejudice, and unwillingness to recognize that the Messiah for whom they had waited so long had now actually come. Even worse perhaps, they faced pagan culture and the might of the Roman Empire, whose ruler was deified and considered the only lord men might properly acknowledge. Acts 12 records an account of the power of the state, as represented in Herod, versus the power of the Word. Luke suggested in this vivid story that even Herod, before whom men prostrated themselves as before God, was but a man of such frailty that in a moment he could be smitten and die. Yet, "the Word of God grew and multiplied" (Acts 12:24).

Kingdoms and empires have risen and faded away. Rulers and tyrants have had their day and perished, but the Word of God abides. God's kingdom continues to invade the earth. Though the power of evil may appear to prevail, a glance back over the centuries reveals that the living Word and the redeeming Christ, whom it reveals, alone abide. As the early disciples discovered, no barrier is too high or too wide to excuse our failure to take that story to all the world.

16—Missions Marks a Momentous Milestone

Acts 13 and 14

One of the most important events in the history of the Christian church occurred in Antioch of Syria somewhere around A.D. 44 or 45. As seen in Acts 11:19, Christians had been scattered by persecution from Jerusalem to various other regions. Some had gone "as far as Phenice and Cyprus, and Antioch."

At Antioch such a great response had been made to the preaching of the word that Barnabas had been sent by the church at Jerusalem to aid in the work. Finding need of assistance, he had gone to Tarsus for Saul (Acts 11:25). Saul and Barnabas together with others, as we shall later see, preached the word, evangelized, and taught the people with great effectiveness. One of the most far-reaching results was a burden by the church to see the gospel proclaimed to the rest of the world also.

The Milestone's Place

Antioch was a significant city at this time. Founded around 300 B.C. by Seleucus Nicator and named for his father Antiochus, Antioch was located on the Orontes River near its entrance into the Mediterranean. The city had become by this time the third largest in the Roman world, exceeded only by Rome and Alexandria. Showing the influence of Roman planning, it possessed splendid streets, impressive buildings, and many statues. Cosmopolitan in character, it attracted people from all parts of the world. At this time it is said to have had at least a half million inhabitants. Many Jews lived there and were accorded the same citizenship rights as were others in the free areas of the empire. Jews and Gentiles, therefore, had greater interchange here perhaps than might have been the case in Jerusalem.

Emil G. Kraeling says the newly instituted Olympics occurred in Antioch in the fall of A.D. 44, bringing thousands of visitors—somewhat as a world's fair of this day—to the city. This added to the opportunity and the challenge of the church there. From this experience Saul may have gained some of his knowledge about athletics which later shows up so frequently in his epistles. Undoubtedly he admired the athletes who had disciplined themselves for the feats in which they were engaged. The apostle would apply this principle again and again to Christian life.

The Power Directing the Venture

Luke tells us what the outside observer could not have seen or understood; namely, that it was the leading of the Holy Spirit which brought about this significant new step toward world missions. "As they ministered to the Lord, and fasted," he writes, "The Holy Ghost said, 'Separate me Barnabas and Saul for the work whereunto I have called them' " (Acts 13:2). The Holy Spirit was laying upon them a burden for the need of the whole world for the message of Christ. The church thus felt compelled to act. We read: "And when they had fasted and prayed, and laid their hands on them, they sent them away" (Acts 13:3).

Strangely, the church at Jerusalem had apparently failed to see, or else to feel, it could carry out the full commission to take the gospel to the uttermost parts of the earth. We are not told whether this was because they were so enjoying their own fellowship or whether they had not felt that the time had as yet come to assume this responsibility.

The record in Acts reveals that it was not easy for the average Jewish member of the early church to overcome his prejudice toward Gentiles and to sense his obligation as a witness to them. It was especially difficult for him to see that others had equal rights to the gospel. Gradually, however, as persecution scattered the church and Gentiles responded to the Holy Spirit, Jewish Christians began more fully to understand the obligation Christ had placed upon them to share the gospel with all men.

The church at Jerusalem apparently did not "fast and pray" concerning its responsibility to send out missionaries as did Antioch. Could this have been a reason also as to why the Holy Spirit chose Antioch for this new step in Christian history? To Antioch, at any rate, fell the honor of being the first church to launch what we now call foreign missions work. Antioch, instead of Jerusalem, thus became the leading center of the world missions task of the early church. Modern church history demonstrates that it is only the missionary church which is the growing church. That church which has the greatest vision of the world and the deepest sense of its own responsibility is the church which is most alive and vigorous. Is this because the Holy Spirit has opportunity in that church which others deny him?

The Persons Most Affected by It

Quite likely, as already said, the whole church at Antioch was caught up with a conviction that the Holy Spirit had laid upon it a responsibility to share the gospel with all nations. Their praying and especially their fasting was in effect an opening of their minds and hearts to the Spirit's directions. These directions were that they should appoint certain of their own brethren to take the good tidings of Jesus Christ to all areas of the empire.

If we may rightly judge from overtones of the account, Saul and Barnabas must have been the leading personalities in the church and perhaps the ones the people most desired to hear. Their decision to send Saul and Barnabas therefore was as though one of our churches today had decided to send its popular pastor and associate to the missions field rather than to hold on to them for their own satisfaction.

Though the Holy Spirit pointed specifically to Barnabas and Saul as the ones whom he would first use in the world missions program now being launched, it is revealed that John Mark was sent also as their minister or attendant.

Much has been made of the fact that Mark later turned back. Paul and Barnabas were to be torn apart over him when he wanted to go with them again and when Barnabas decided to give him a second chance. Whatever may have been the reason for Paul's disappointment in Mark, we are glad that before Paul's death John Mark had so proven himself to win Paul's fullest confidence.

Paul was likely a younger man than Barnabas, but Barnabas was an outstanding personality. He was given recognition above Paul at first. The endearing name Barnabas (meaning "son of encouragement") had been given him by his brethren. Soon Paul, however, rose to the place of leadership.

The Program Which Issued from It

There seems to have been no specific plan revealed by the Holy Spirit to the early church as to how it should launch the world missions undertaking which it was now impressed to assume. Neither is there any mention that the church even thought it necessary to provide financial support, but it may have given some help anyway. Paul would later tell us that he labored with his own hands to take care of his expenses. The church, however, gave these representatives something more valuable than money. It sent them with its concern and prayers. Only after it had "fasted and prayed" did it lay hands upon them and send them out.

There was no mission board to support or guide Barnabas and Paul. The Holy Spirit alone would daily sustain and lead them. This is not to deny the need in our day of mission boards. Through these the churches can now cooperatively provide resources and channel their concern to help sustain and guide their representatives as these take the gospel elsewhere.

The apostles felt impressed by the Holy Spirit first to go to Seleucia and thence to sail to Cyprus. They preached the word at Salamis in the synagogues of the Jews and went through the isle of Paphos proclaiming the gospel.

Barnabas was a native of Cyprus. One wonders whether this might have had some influence on his desire to go there. To assume such is obviously not to deny at the same time the Holy Spirit's leading of these missionaries. Those who cannot take the gospel to their own homes and homelands are hardly competent to take it elsewhere.

Paul and Barnabas felt in the will of the Spirit that they should proclaim the gospel from city to city. Ultimately they went to Perga in Pamphylia (where John Mark turned back) and later to another Antioch, in Pisidia. The preaching of these missionaries placed emphasis on the history of the Jews and the fulfilment of that history in the coming, the death, and the resurrection of Christ. Response was usually made by both Jew and Gentile. The Jews soon became envious, however, and began to contradict and blaspheme Paul. At this point (Acts 13:46) one of the remarkable turns in the history of Christianity is recorded: "Then Paul and Barnabas waxed bold, and said, 'It was necessary that the word of God should first have been spoken to you; but seeing ye put it from you, and judge yourselves unworthy of everlasting life, lo, we turn to the Gentiles.' "

The program in this early stage of world missions was not essentially unlike that of today. It basically involved teaching the word to all who would listen, proclaiming the good news of the gospel, interpreting the meaning of God's redemptive purpose in Christ, and ministering in love to the needs of men. From the chapters presently under study, it may be noted how carefully the messengers unfolded to their hearers the redemptive plan God had followed across the centuries. They proclaimed Jesus as Saviour and Lord and as the only hope of men. They taught the meaning of Christian service and stewardship. They evidently organized a church in each place where a group of believers could be assembled. We are told that upon their return through the cities where they had earlier witnessed, they appointed pastors and leaders to take care of these congregations and thus sought to strengthen the churches in every way possible. These are still basically the same ministries which churches today perform in all the world.

The Progress Attendant upon It

That the Holy Spirit was with them and brought about results wherever Paul and Barnabas engaged in missionary service is apparent. Though opposition by the Jews gradually stiffened, many of them were led to become believers. The Gentiles apparently responded in considerable numbers. We are told that multitudes waited upon the ministry of these missionaries.

Paul concluded that the gospel was to be given to the Gentiles, not only from the terms of his own call (Acts 9:15) but also from the prophetic declaration (Isa. 49:6), indicating that this was in God's longstanding purpose. When the Gentiles heard the gospel was especially to be proclaimed to them, they were glad and glorified God and many believed (Acts 13:48). Significantly, it is added, "And the word of the Lord was published throughout all the region." Believers became sowers. Those who had felt the impact and the change made in them by the power of Jesus Christ became witnesses of Christ themselves. It is little wonder, therefore, that with great exhilaration and joy Paul and Barnabas brought a thrilling message back to Antioch of ". . . all that God had done with them, and how he had opened the door of faith unto the Gentiles" (Acts 14:27).

17 — History's First Foreign Missions Conference

Acts 15:1-35

The multiplied conferences and conventions of today often become a weariness of the flesh. What good after all do they accomplish? The far-reaching influence of the conference described in Acts 15 suggests such conferences may be wise expenditures of energy and time. "Reading maketh a full man," said Francis Bacon, "conference a ready man." Only eternity will fully reveal how much the conference of the group assembled in Jerusalem, probably sometime in the year A.D. 50, has meant to the cause of Christian missions.

The Prelude to It—a Problem

Not greatly unlike the reasons for many conferences now, this one dealt with a problem of vital importance which had arisen in the church at Antioch. Acts 15:1 reads: "And certain men which came down from Judea taught the brethren, and said, 'Except ye be circumcised after the manner of Moses, ye cannot be saved.' " These men were Pharisees who had become Christians, but had evidently not as yet been fully enlightened concerning how much or how little of the Mosiac law the Christian was obliged to fulfil. Though they had acknowledged Christ as Saviour, they felt it essential to continue observance of certain Jewish rites. They therefore saw salvation as resting not entirely on the grace of God, but as requiring at least the fulfilment of the Jewish law of circumcision.

This view was like the argument made today by some that, for salvation one must not only believe in Jesus Christ as Lord and Saviour, but he must also be baptized.

The sect of the Pharisees was creating a great stir in the church over this issue. Paul and Barnabas, it is said, "had no small dissension and disputation with them" (Acts 15:2). Obviously, a disagreement between the missionaries and those who had recently come from Jerusalem could not help but affect the church. But it was soon decided that the issue should be settled soon and once for all.

The Preparation for It

Perhaps at a conference the church decided to send Paul and Barnabas with certain other members of the congregation to Jerusalem to meet with the apostles and elders for a discussion of this question. In effect, the members were appointing messengers to represent the church in the conference and to bring back a decision for their guidance. It should be noted, however, that they anticipated only a conference in Jerusalem and not a handing down of a decree from some authority.

The church at Antioch was thoughtful this time of the needs of their representatives. Acts 15:3 is best translated: "They therefore having been furnished with the requisites for the journey by the assembly [church], proceeded on their way." Funds were likely provided for the journey.

This was not, however, to be a mere journey up to Jerusalem and back, but an opportunity also for continued witness and missionary service. The group went through Phoenicia, which was Gentile territory lying on the Mediterranean coast south of what is now Lebanon, and then on through Samaria, the area which the typical non-Christian Jew of that day would have avoided because of its mixed population. In each of these, news of the conversion of Gentiles elsewhere brought great rejoicing among those who had already believed. Churches had previously been established in these areas obviously by believers who had been scattered earlier from Jerusalem by persecution. Unlike too many who journey in this day to church gatherings, forgetting the opportunities afforded on the way for missionary work, Paul and Barnabas and their associates neglected no opportunity for winning men to Christ.

The Place of It

As already noted, Paul and Barnabas and the others from Antioch had been commissioned to take up the problem which had arisen among them with the church, and especially the apostles, at Jerusalem. Although Antioch had now become the leading center for foreign missions endeavor, Jerusalem continued to have a major influence. This was due to the presence of such leaders as Peter, James (Jesus' brother), and John, and perhaps several others of the original group of disciples. This is not to say, however, that Jerusalem considered itself the "mother" church and thus to have authority over other congregations elsewhere. Apparently Antioch recognized that those who had personally been taught by Christ would be the best advisors on an issue of such serious consequences as that which had arisen. Interestingly, the leaders at Jerusalem now seem to have centered more on James than on Peter or the other apostles.

How many of the brethren in Jerusalem gathered for the conference with the group from Antioch we are not told. It is said though that those who had come from Antioch "were received of the church, and of the apostles and elders" (Acts 15:4), suggesting not merely a private conference with the apostles but also a full church meeting. Possibly after a general discussion of the issue brought before the body, there was a further meeting in which the apostles and elders came together "to consider of this matter" (Acts 15:6). Whether this supposition is valid or not, it is obvious from Acts 15:5 that there were some from Antioch in the gathering at Jerusalem. When it is remembered how often the Pharisees fell under the condemnation of Christ for their restrictive attitudes, one may be surprised that apparently a considerable number of Pharisees were now members of the church. The point of view taken by these converted Pharisees concerning observance of certain traditional rites should not, however, be surprising.

The Program Pursued by It

Unlike our well-ordered conventions or conferences of this day with their program participants scheduled in advance, the meeting at Jerusalem had no previously prepared order to follow. When gathered, the church heard the testimony of Paul and Barnabas about what had been wrought through them on their great missionary journey. Obviously, also the issue which had arisen at Antioch was reported to the church as were the difficulties it posed.

Almost at once those who belonged to the sect of the Pharisees in Jerusalem began to defend the position their brethren had been advocating at Antioch.

The whole conference, though tense and sometimes given to heated discussion, seems to have been marked by democratic orderliness, by reverence, and by respect for one another. It was also characterized by deep seriousness. Undoubtedly, many of those present could see how important the issue before them had become. The time had arrived for it to be thrashed out satisfactorily. Apparently, the church was unhurried in its deliberations. We are told: "And when there had been much disputing" [better translated "a long debate"] (Acts 15:7), Peter took the floor for his testimony. In debate, full freedom was afforded for anyone to speak who wanted to discuss the issue. It is obvious that neither Peter nor anyone else sought to dominate or to dictate the conclusions which were to be reached.

Ultimately, Peter was moved, however, to bear his own testimony as to what God had done through him in reaching Gentiles with the gospel. He insisted that God had made no difference between Jew and Gentile and that the Holy Spirit had worked in each alike to bring about conviction and lead to salvation. He pleaded that no yoke be placed about the necks of the Gentiles. He proclaimed, moreover, that the Gentile, like the Jew, is saved through grace (the undeserved favor and mercy of the Lord Jesus) (Acts 15:11). The impact of Peter's testimony was so profound that it left the congregation apparently in breathless silence. Everyone remained silent until Barnabas and Paul felt moved to relate their own experience publicly as to the signs and wonders which God had wrought through them among the Gentiles.

The testimony of Peter followed by the witness of Barnabas and Paul had a telling effect. But it was the wisdom of James which brought the conference to its climax. James set forth from the prophets, especially from Amos, Jeremiah, and Isaiah, the argument that it had always been God's purpose to reach the Gentiles as well as the Jews (Acts 15:15-18). The respect given James by those assembled in the conference is indicated by how influential his opinions were upon the body. "Wherefore my sentence is" (Acts 15:19) is better translated "wherefore my judgment is" or "wherefore my opinion is." He was not pronouncing an edict or giving a verdict, but stating conviction.

Prevailing Decision Reached by It

What James recommended apparently even convinced those present with a Pharisaic background, for a unanimous decision was given by the congregation concerning his recommendation. James advised that no obstacle be put in the way of Gentile believers and no cause of disturbance or confusion be allowed in the work of the church. James was saying that men are saved by grace through faith and not by keeping of certain religious rites. To this judgment he added only the advice that word be sent to Antioch and to the churches elsewhere that believers abstain from the "pollutions of the idols, and from fornication, and from things strangled, and from blood" (Acts 15:20). These were practical considerations to help guard the influence of Christians and to keep the world from confusing Christian practices with those in the pagan temples.

Significantly, there seems to have been total agreement and even joy in the conclusion to which James' counsel brought the whole discussion. We are told that what he advised pleased not only the apostles and elders but also the whole church.

To relieve Barnabas and Paul, the assembly sent some of its own company back to Antioch to bear the decisions of the conference and to convey their greetings.

It is significant that a written statement was prepared by the conference, which forever set the matter on record so as to leave no doubt concerning the conclusion reached. The decision or letter itself may have been drafted by the hand of James. Some of his own unique wording at least found its way into the communication.

The news which came out of the conference at Jerusalem brought great joy and consolation to the church at Antioch and to churches elsewhere throughout the areas reached by the missionaries. The courageous and historic decision which had been made was cause enough for joy; but that joy was perhaps enhanced by the commendations also sent concerning "our beloved Barnabas and Paul, men who have hazarded their lives in the name of our Lord Jesus Christ" (Acts 15:25-26). The Jerusalem conference let it be known that it stood fully behind these great missionaries and left no question anywhere as to the complete endorsement of the message these missionaries were bearing.

18—Missions Maturing and Multiplying

Acts 15:36 to 17:15

After the historic conference in Jerusalem, as recorded in Acts 15:1-29, Paul, Barnabas, and the others from Antioch and Jerusalem hurried to Antioch with the joyous news about decisions reached there. For sometime thereafter, Paul and Barnabas remained in that city teaching and preaching the word as they had done before their first great missionary tour. Paul, in time, became burdened, however, to know how the churches established on the first tour were progressing. Hence he proposed to Barnabas that they make a visit to every city where they had formerly preached the word.

Multiplying by Division

Paul's proposal led to an unexpected development. Barnabas desired to take Mark with them. This brought dismay to Paul, as the latter had been grievously disappointed by Mark's turning back at Pamphylia on the first tour. Why Mark did this is never specifically stated, but the reason was evidently disappointing and seemed inexcusable to Paul. Mark appeared to be a quitter. Among people only recently converted an example of steadfastness was thought by Paul to be an imperative. A sharp division arose between Paul and Barnabas which was sadly to separate them. Paul decided to take Silas with him, and Barnabas set off to Cyprus with John Mark.

The account of the division between Paul and Barnabas is a reminder that even great men, including missionaries such as Paul and Barnabas, are still human. The grace of God, however, can overrule such weaknesses and cause even their divisions to extend the work of the church. The later account in the New Testament regarding Paul and Barnabas encourages the belief that true Christians will eventually find ways of rebuilding a fellowship which has been severed. This certainly turned out to be the case with these two immortal missionaries.

Mark was a relative of Barnabas, either a cousin or a nephew. This fact may have led Barnabas to take a stand in behalf of Mark, but Barnabas was by nature the type person more likely to give a man a second chance than Paul. Paul did mention Barnabas afterward as a notable missionary working under the same motivation as himself (1 Cor. 9:6). Mark also in time completely rewon the confidence of Paul (2 Tim. 4:11). From this point onward, Luke focused his story on the life and labors of Paul. One could wish someone had given a similar account of the ministry of Barnabas. Luke's story seems to follow a plan showing how the Great Commission was carried out by proclamation of the gospel in Jerusalem, Judea, Samaria, and then to the uttermost parts of the earth. Luke had a special reason for following the course of Paul's career. He was to become a participant, as we shall later see, in the work of Paul and was thus personally informed about it.

Multiplying Through Selection of a Teammate

Paul and Silas, we are told, "departed, being recommended by the brethren unto the grace of God" (Acts 15:40), and proceeded through Syria and Cilicia, then moved on to Derbe and Lystra. At the latter, Timothy entered the picture. Son of a Jewish mother and a Greek father, he had already become a Christian and was an effective witness in his area, being "well reported of by the brethren that were at Lystra and Iconium" (Acts 16:2). The best endorsement of any man for missionary work is how much he is doing at home.

Derbe had been the farthest point to which Paul had gone on the first missionary journey. The congregation of believers formed there must have welcomed his return. It was at Lystra, however, that Paul received "a gift from heaven," in the enlistment of Timothy.

The Lycaonian area of Derbe and Lystra at that time was a rather forbidding region, less civilized than anywhere else Paul had ministered. Fewer Jews had come to the area, and apparently no Jewish synagogue existed in either city. Here Paul had to begin his work by preaching to the heathen. Tradition has it that Timothy had been converted on Paul's first misisonary tour there. Paul was later to refer to him as his "son in the faith" (1 Tim. 1:2). As Timothy was a young man of considerable promise, it is not surprising to read, "him would Paul have to go forth with him" (Acts 16:3).

To help Timothy to be accepted by the Jews, Paul thought he should accept the Hebrew rite of circumcision. This may seem surprising especially in view of the decision reached a short while earlier in the Jerusalem conference. Paul would have no one believe that any rite was essential to salvation. He nonetheless saw no wrong in Timothy's conforming to the rite in question if it would remove prejudice against him by the Jews who knew him to be the son of a Greek father.

Multiplying by Strengthening the Churches

As this team of three—Paul, Timothy, and Silas—now moved on through the cities of that region, they delivered the Jerusalem decree and sought to strengthen the organization and ministry of each church. The result was reported by Luke (Acts 16:5) as a daily increase. The work of evangelism and missionary witness was bearing its constant fruit. Pressing on with their witness, the team went throughout the region of Phrygia and Galatia, possibly the northernmost part to which Paul's witness was borne. For some reason the missionaries were "forbidden of the Holy Ghost to preach the word in Asia" (Acts 16:6). Though Paul may have gone on to Antioch (in Asia Minor), this is not mentioned. Asia as used in the above expression meant the area around Ephesus, then the chief city of the region and the end of the east-west highway through Asia Minor. Why the Holy Spirit forbade the visit of the missionaries to this important area to which Paul evidently wanted to go has been left a mystery. Instead of going there, they were to bear the gospel to the Galatian territory where the "barbarians" lived. These were non-Greeks and a people little influenced by Greek culture, and thus people to whom Paul would naturally have been less inclined to go. The Holy Spirit, however, wanted the message preached there, too.

Later the misisonaries moved on to Mysia and wanted also to go to Bithynia, but again "the Spirit suffered them not" (Acts 16:7). A more far-reaching step was now about to be taken, one of the most significant in all the history of missionary activity.

Multiplying by Response to the Macedonian Call

In the coastal town of Troas on the Aegean Sea, Paul had a vision of historical consequence. Here he saw a man of Macedonia praying, "Come over into Macedonia, and help us" (Acts 16:9). Macedonia formed the eastern shore of Europe. Later penetration by the gospel into all of Europe stemmed from the vision at Troas!

Greek language and culture had already greatly affected Paul and were useful to him in all his ministry. Though Rome had conquered Greece, Greece had in a sense conquered Rome with its superior civilization. Greek civilization combined with Roman military genius and law, from a human standpoint, seemed to have everything but Christ. Lacking him, it had nothing to Paul of eternal worth.

One can only imagine how the great mind and vision of Paul were captivated by the thought of bearing the gospel to the Western world. With rising pulse and quickened anticipation, he likely sensed that the Spirit was now leading him to make the decisive step of moving from East to West with the word.

One should note at this point the entrance of the pronouns *we* and *us* into the account in Acts.

At Troas or near there, Luke the physician joined the missionary team. That team was composed thereafter for some time of four—Paul, Silas, Timothy, and Luke. It would appear from the account that Luke considered himself a missionary, too. Such seems to be the meaning of his statement, "assuredly gathering that the Lord had called us for to preach the gospel unto them" (Acts 16:10). Though we are not told that Luke performed any medical service on the missionary tour, it was he who wrote Acts. His modesty would have kept him from mentioning his own work. It is not too much to suppose, therefore, that he did perform certain medical services and thus was in reality the first medical missionary in the history of the church.

Soon the team was in Philippi where several well-known events took place. The first person won to Christ there was Lydia, a native of Thyatira in Asia Minor to which Paul had been only recently forbidden to go! Lydia was carrying on an important business in the city. The purple cloth of Thyatira was popular in that day and was in considerable demand by the wealthy as a status symbol. Lydia and the women associated with her—perhaps servants or women in her employ—made at least a small audience by the riverside for the preaching of the gospel the first time it was publicly proclaimed in the Western world. Strangely, the "man in Macedonia" Paul had seen turned out to be a woman, or several women!

The next woman who enters the account was a poor slave girl, exploited by merciless businessmen for gain. Her conversion caused a business loss to her owners, and this could not be tolerated. "And when her masters saw that the hope of their gains was gone, they caught Paul and Silas, and drew them into the marketplace unto the rulers" (Acts 16:19). We do not know why Luke and Timothy were not also arrested. Possibly they were Greek in appearance, while Paul and Silas were Jewish and were thus assumed not to be Roman citizens. That assumption was to prove embarrassing. Despite the pain they must have suffered from the stripes with which they had been beaten, they were still bearing a witness. A witness like that in a prison dungeon will have its effect. That night when the earthquake came and the bands of the prisoners were loosed, nobody atempted to flee. A further consequence was the conversion of the Philippian jailer and of his household. How many were included, we do not know. But the gospel was still bearing its fruit.

Multiplying by Witness in Thessalonica and Berea

After being delivered from prison and returning to the house of Lydia, "when they had seen the brethren" (Acts 16:40) (that is, the other believers in the city), the missionary team departed to Thessalonica. Following his custom, Paul entered the synagogue on the sabbath and reasoned out of the Scriptures with the Jews there, "alleging, that Christ must needs have suffered, and risen again from the dead; and that this Jesus, whom I preach unto you, is Christ" (Acts 17:3). Here converts in considerable number among religious-minded Greeks especially, and "of the chief women not a few" (Acts 17:4), accepted their witness. As had been true from the beginning in Jerusalem, however, there were other Jews who closed their minds to the message brought by the missionaries and, "moved with envy" (Acts 17:5), stirred up a mob in opposition. Paul and Silas, likely accompanied by Timothy and Luke, though they are not mentioned, moved on to Berea. A similar response to their message is reported in that city. Here "many . . . honourable women which were Greeks, and of men, not a few" believed (Acts 17:12).

Thus the fruit of misisonary service continued to multiply. From Jerusalem the gospel had not only reached Judea and Samaria but was also truly penetrating the uttermost parts of the earth.

Typical of the preaching which these missionaries must have done was the simple message given by Paul to the Philippian jailor: "Believe on the Lord Jesus Christ, and thou shalt be saved" (Acts 16:31).

In our time of growing metropolises and megalopolises, with their frightful and complex needs, Christians need a new vision of what was discovered in the long ago; namely, the power of the gospel truly to transform the city and the world.

19—Missions in Cultural and Commercial Capitals

Acts 17:15 to 18:21

Standing before the churches like a yawning and frightening chasm is the problem of the city. No Christian denomination seems at present to be adequately coping with this problem. Many, including Southern Baptists, appear to be baffled by its demands.

One of the major crises of this age centers in the city. Warner B. Ragsdale, Jr., a specialist on urban affairs, writes: "Rebuilding America's cities isn't merely a matter of bricks and mortar, or even money. New ways must be found to change the lives of millions of people."

Such statements would by no means have sounded strange in the ears of the apostle Paul. He saw the need for getting the gospel to as many people everywhere as possible. He saw an even greater urgency of proclaiming it in great metropolitan centers where the crosscurrents of life constantly met.

Jerusalem, the hub of the Jewish world of that day, Antioch of Syria, Ephesus, Philippi, Athens, and Corinth were all centers of world influence. The Holy Spirit evidently directed the first great Christian missionaries to concentrate on the great cities of their day. These cosmopolitan centers were places of great need and opportunity for the spread of the gospel. Strategy employed by early missionaries proved to be gloriously fruitful. The story of how, despite growing persecution, the Christian witness spread over the Roman empire and beyond is nothing short of miraculous.

People tend to desert the complex, sometimes repulsive, and often decaying centers of population and flee to the more affluent and attractive climate of suburbia. The suburbs need the gospel, too; but no amount of activity in suburbia can relieve the church of its obligation for the people of the inner city.

Burdened to bear the gospel to as many cities as possible, Paul pressed on against every handicap. We have already seen how he came to Philippi and how a church was born as a consequence of this visit. We have followed him from Philippi to Thessalonica and then to Berea where in each place believers were baptized by churches.

After all this, Luke informs us, "And they that conducted Paul brought him unto Athens" (Acts 17:15).

Missions in the Cultural Capital of the World

What quickening of pulse Paul must have felt as he laid eyes on this famous city for the first time. Scholar that he was, he would have been acquainted with the great philosophers who had already made Athens famous. Being, perhaps, a product of the university of Tarsus, he was also familiar with the university then in Athens. The university at Alexandria by this time outshone Athens in some respects, such as in scientific and literary work. But Athens was still recognized as the leading philosophic center of the world.

Many have taken a dim view of Paul's preaching at Athens. Some have even charged Paul with playing up to the intellectuals of the city rather than proclaiming, as his custom was elsewhere, the simplicities of the gospel. A comment of Paul's to the church at Corinth is thought to support this view: "And I, brethren," he later wrote, "when I came to you, came not with excellency of speech or of wisdom, declaring unto you the testimony of God. For I determined not to know anything among you, save Jesus Christ, and him crucified" (1 Cor. 2:1-2). This statement has been taken to mean that Paul had learned a lesson in Athens and had resolved to change his approach in Corinth. But this is a doubtful interpretation. The truth is that Paul preached a great sermon there—one of such historic significance that it has affected the thinking of most of the civilized world ever since.

The results of Paul's sermon and personal work in Athens cannot be considered small. Similar results in an intellectual center of renown today would be considered highly significant.

Paul evidently realized that the leaders of thought in this world center of culture could have tremendous influence upon all the world. The brilliant mind of the apostle naturally would have grasped the importance of a witness in a place like this. We may wonder whether Christians today understand the importance of a similar missionary outreach to centers of learning.

Paul sensed that the various philosophies proclaimed in Athens offered salvation for no one. Christ, crucified and risen, alone afforded both life and the only sound understanding of life. In a day of different beliefs, Christians dare not forget the urgent importance of outthinking the rest of the world as did their early Christian counterparts. "The whole world is in danger," someone has said, "when God lets loose a thinker." Instead of the world's being endangered, the reverse of this could be true, if only that thinker were of the persuasion of a Paul or an Augustine, a Roger Williams or a William Carey. Through literature and every other means of communication, we must strive to reach the minds as well as the souls of men.

Athens, though not as full of grandeur as at an earlier period, was still remarkable (as it is today) for its impressive buildings, its beautiful gardens, and its many temples. As Paul viewed these his heart grew sick, however, with the realization that the temples were erected to heathen gods.

Finding a temple one day on which were the words, "To the unknown God," Paul, with his brilliant understanding of the problem faced in Athens, realized he now had a cue with which to address the city. In his introductory statement at Mars Hill, Paul said, therefore, "I perceive that in all things you are too superstitous" (Acts 17:22), meaning, "I observe you are very religious." Recalling the temple named for the "unknown God," Paul continued, "Whom therefore ye ignorantly worship, him declare I unto you" (Acts 17:23). He followed this proclamation with the setting forth of certain great and eternal truths about God and man which must have set many of his listeners on a new course of thinking, and, as already indicated, which also have had a bearing on human thought ever since.

Paul declared that the God who made all things has not confined himself to temples made with hands. Nor can men adequately serve him merely by what they do with their hands. God is not dependent upon men for anything. Instead, he is the source himself of "life, and breath, and all things" (Acts 17:25). Philosophy reaches its highest conception when it understands, as Paul proclaimed, that God is the author of all creation.

The second great principle set forth in Paul's sermon was that the Creator has made "of one blood all nations of men for to dwell on all the face of the earth" (Acts 17:26).

We are still struggling, even in the most civilized parts of the world to come to grips with this truth. Before God, all racial and other barriers must be overcome.

Paul further affirmed that God so ordered the circumstances surrounding men as to influence them to seek him. The true God of creation, furthermore, is not far from every one of us. He is the very source of life. In him men move and have their being. This even some of the wisest in Athens had already come to understand.

The statement "We are the offspring of God" (Acts 17:29) is not to be interpreted as meaning that Paul proclaimed a physical descent from God by man, but rather to emphasize that man is the creative work of God. This is another way of saying that we are made in God's image and likeness.

The climax of Paul's great sermon was to inform the hearers that the "times of this ignorance [man's turning to gods made by human hands, etc.] God winked at [or overlooked]; but now commandeth all men everywhere to repent" (Acts 17:30).

The need of repentance was further underscored by Paul's declaration that there is an appointed day for judgment in which God will judge the world in righteousness by "that man whom he hath ordained; whereof he hath given assurance unto all men, in that he hath raised him from the dead" (Acts 17:31). Until Paul reached this point, he undoubtedly had a captivated audience. When he mentioned resurrection from the dead, however, most of those listening to him found this beyond belief. Some mocked, but others wanted to hear more.

Why Paul decided to depart from Athens soon after his sermon at Mars Hill is not known. We do know, however, that a group "clave unto him" (Acts 17:34); and a number believed. Among these were two prominent people, Dionysius the Areopagite and a woman named Damaris. There is no record that a church was organized in Athens at this time, but Paul was able to leave behind a group who in time would form a congregation of believers and would further make known the gospel in that needy city.

Missions in the Commercial Capital of Prominence

Leaving Athens, Paul moved on to Corinth. Corinth was a city strategically located and of great affluence. The city had existed for two or possibly three thousand years before Paul's visit. Its position on the isthmus between the northern part of the Greek mainland and the Peloponnesus on the south made it a bridge for commerce between the East and the West. It had a harbor on both sides of its narrow strip and had been a busy maritime center for ages. Though Rome had destroyed it in 146 B.C., it had been rebuilt under Caesar and was again flourishing.

Though a canal now exists near Corinth, making possible the passage of ships from the Aegean Sea to the western gulf of Lechaeum, in that day cargo was hauled from one shoreline to the other across the neck of land on which the city stood. Smaller ships often were transported on rollers across this land bridge. It is difficult to conceive how important the city was at that time. But its wealth and prosperity were exceeded only by its sin and idolatry. The reading of Paul's letters to the Corinthians will serve to inform one of how great the struggle was, even with early Christians there, to overcome the harmful influence of the culture in which they lived. Paul was confident, however, that the risen and triumphant Christ he proclaimed could transform men even in this pagan, immoral atmosphere. Though they were wedded to pleasure and to every form of vice and immoral practice, Christ could make them new.

At one time, according to records, more than one thousand young women in Corinth gave themselves to ritualistic prostitution in the temple worship of that city. Athens, despite all its intellectual sophistication, obviously needed Christ. Corinth, with all its corruption, also needed him. Moreover, the many who came and went through the city, if they could only hear the gospel, might take it to all parts of the civilized world.

The vision and courage of Paul and his fellow missionaries, as they undertook the task of establishing a church at Corinth, were notable and far-reaching. The Corinthian letters alone are convincing evidence as to how great the impact of this mighty work really was.

The missionary undertaking of the church today can never be completed—indeed it cannot be seriously set forward—without attention to both the intellectual and the commercial centers of the world. These places where patterns of human thought are formed, great movements of life are in constant flux, and influences are generated which affect the whole world, constitute possibly the greatest challenge with which Christians are confronted.

20—Missionary Agony and Ecstasy

Acts 18:18 to 21:14

Although a superficial reading of Acts 18:18 to Acts 21:14 does not clearly reveal it, the period covered by this passage possibly marks the most productive and effective years in the entire ministry of the apostle Paul.

Paul had a glorious ministry in Corinth, a great commercial center at the crossroads of the world of that day. Most likely during this stay there he had also written 1 Thessalonians, the first book, it is thought, to be included in the New Testament.

In the statement in Acts 18:18, "And Paul after this tarried there yet a good while," there is indicated an extensive ministry in Corinth even beyond the disturbance reported in Acts 18:12-17. His ministry in this city, in fact, lasted as long as two years. However, he felt led to move on to Ephesus, another great center of world significance in that time.

Priscilla and Aquila, with whom Paul had made his home during his days in Corinth, decided to go with him to Ephesus. Paul left them there after a brief visit with the assurance that he would return. He then made a special trip to Jerusalem, passing through Caesarea. He also went to Antioch from which church he had gone out as a missionary. Likely he felt impelled to bring a report to and confer with the apostles in Jerusalem as well as with the leaders at Antioch.

Following his visits in Caesarea, Jerusalem, and Antioch Paul decided (Acts 18:23) to return through areas where he had traveled on earlier missionary journeys. It is never enough merely to establish churches and to see that they get off to a good start. Further support and guidance are always desirable and usually needed.

Joys and Satisfaction of the Missionary

Paul, like many other missionaries, must have found great joy and satisfaction from some of the events already mentioned. For example, the good news brought him by Silas and Timothy concerning the growth and faithfulness of the Thessalonians (Acts 18:5) was a reward of great meaning. He had been burdened and fearful about that church (1 Thess. 3:1). Now he could say: "For now we live, if ye stand fast in the Lord" (1 Thess. 3:8).

A further satisfaction must have come to the great apostle from his being able to report both to the church at Jerusalem and to the church at Antioch what miracles and wonders God had wrought through the ministry of himself and his associates. The world significance of reaching Athens and Corinth with the gospel could readily have been recognized by all who heard the account.

A special joy and reward for any missionary is undoubtedly to revisit fields where his own work has led to the establishment of churches now well on their way to larger usefulness. It takes little imagination to conceive how each of these young churches Paul revisited was inspired and challenged by the report the apostle brought as to the preaching of the gospel elsewhere. These congregations would have been made aware of the larger fellowship now being extended even across other continents and of the mutual love and prayerful concern of growing hosts of people. Their opportunity to consult with the apostle, furthermore, about their own needs and plans must have been for them a highly rewarding experience.

Yet another source of joy and satisfaction for Paul was to know of the continuing work of dependable and committed lay people like Priscilla and Aquila, whom Paul had left behind in Ephesus. Paul had likely lived in their home during his work in Corinth and had been associated with them in the tent-making business. He had also interpreted the gospel to them. An instance of the value of this instruction is revealed in Acts 18:24-28. A young Jew by the name of Apollos, born in Alexandria, Egypt, and possibly educated in the famous university there, a man of eloquence and ability, had come to Ephesus before Paul's return. There he began to preach. But his knowledge of the word had certain defects. What he had come to know about the Scriptures was perhaps weighted toward the traditional Hebrew interpretation. Aquila and Priscilla quietly and effectively were able to teach him and guide him into fuller truth. Apollos was humble and receptive enough, despite his natural ability and education, to learn from these lay people.

How pleased Paul must have been when he finally returned to Ephesus and learned how effective this splendid lay couple had been in guiding Apollos. Apollos was later to go on to Corinth, where he continued the ministry begun there by Paul and was apparently most effective. About a year after having left Ephesus, Paul returned (Acts 19:1). Not even the apostle, perhaps, could foresee how significant his ministry here would soon become.

Like Corinth, Ephesus was a great commercial center and one of the main provincial capitals of the Roman Empire. Situated at the junction of important natural trade routes, it had become far-famed as the whereabouts of the shrine to the nature goddess, Artemis. Its famous temple was massive and impressive. Its theater, moreover, was one of the largest of all that remained from that period. The city had a staduim also which seated some twenty-six thousand. Its spiritual need, however, was exceedingly great.

Problems and Burdens of the Missionary

One of the first things Paul encountered as he returned to Ephesus was a misguided, or else ill-informed, group of believers. These people had been led to accept a viewpoint about Jesus Christ which was not adequate. They claimed they had never even heard of the Holy Spirit. Paul found it essential to correct their misinformation and to lead them to full commitment to Christ and to a surrender to the work of the Holy Spirit within them. How often a like ministry has been needed on missions fields since that day.

For three months Paul boldly preached in the Jewish synagogue of Ephesus. Soon, however, as so often occurred, a current of opposition among the Jews developed against him.

On Paul's earlier misisonary tour he had felt that the Holy Spirit had forbidden him to go to Ephesus and had directed him rather to move from Troas to Europe. Now he was convinced that the Spirit wanted him to minister in Ephesus. When opposition developed, he felt he must find another way to continue his preaching of the gospel there (Acts 19:9). He was able to rent a hall, used evidently in the mornings for school purposes, to which thousands were able to come for daily discussions and sermons by him. The fame of his preaching spread. The commercial character of the city naturally drew many from that region and beyond to the city.

These in turn were undoubtedly captivated by the news which they heard from this brilliant and devout missionary.

For two whole years Paul pursued his work at Ephesus. One can only imagine the throngs who must have been touched by it.

Resistance to the work of missions can never be an adequate excuse for stopping. With Paul, when one approach failed or was prohibited, another was sought. Sometimes such interference proves to be a blessing in disguise. This was true at Ephesus. It is hardly conceivable that the gospel would ever have resulted in the significant reach and impact it had in that region if its proclamation had been confined to the synagogue where Paul began to preach.

A sidelight upon the impact made in Ephesus by the ministry of Paul is given in the story about the seven sons of Sceva, a Jew and a chief priest. These sons were engaged in the superstitious practice of casting out evil spirits. They were so taken by the effect of Paul's preaching that they began to capitalize on his influence for their own ends. They sought to cast out evil spirits by using the formula: "We adjure you by Jesus whom Paul preaches" (Acts 19:13). Soon, however, the hypocrisy of their practice was detected; and they were given a sound beating. Though neither the conduct of these sons of Sceva nor the revenge taken on them could have been pleasing to Paul, the result was that his ministry was all the more magnified.

One of the most impressive consequences of the event just mentioned, and indeed of the whole work of Paul in this pagan city, was the discovery by the people of how they had been deceived by magic and superstition. Their disillusionment was so sweeping that many brought their books on magic and burned them in the sight of all.

We are not told that Paul approved of the book burning, but he must have been pleased to see the people giving up magic and heathen superstitutions and turning to the gospel. Luke impressively recorded, "So mightily grew the word of God and prevailed" (Acts 19:20).

About this time, Paul felt impressed of the Spirit to move on from his labors in Ephesus and again visit churches in Macedonia and Achaia. He also planned other visits to Jerusalem and to Rome (Acts 19:21). Paul's interest in Rome was not the curiosity of a tourist but instead his knowledge of the strategic importance of this empire city.

Before Paul could leave Ephesus, however, trouble of a serious nature arose. A group whose business was making silver shrines for the worship of Artemis began to see the adverse impact of the preaching of the gospel on this business. Soon the whole city was shaken by the uproar they stirred up. Paul himself was persuaded to stay away from the tumult. Some scholars, however, think far more happened than is recorded in Acts. Quite likely Luke, not having been with Paul at Ephesus, only summarizes the major developments there. Many think Paul referred to this period when in his letter to Corinth he wrote, "of much affliction and anguish of heart . . . with many tears" (2 Cor. 2:4).

Some think Paul was imprisoned in Ephesus for a time and that it was during this imprisonment that several of his letters were written. We do know he wrote 1 and 2 Corinthians there. These letters reveal some of the grave problems at Corinth which likely caused the apostle much grief. Such a statement as "without were fightings, within were fears" (2 Cor. 7:5) seems to be an echo of the heartbreak of the apostle.

Despite all the successes which attended his labors, burdens of vast and serious nature fell upon him. These, however, were used of God to bring forth from his mind and heart some of the richest material in the New Testament. This material continues to serve as a guide for Christian development and reaches beyond anything modern pen has ever set down.

Following the nerve-racking and fearsome disturbance caused by the business interests related to the shrines of Artemis, Paul sent for the disciples. Having warned them, he then proceeded on his journey to Macedonia and on to Greece. In the latter, he spent three months. Soon another plot was formed against him. A gathering storm of opposition, especially from the Jews, was indeed spreading from place to place and was possibly forming throughout the empire. Forewarnings of cost and danger to his ministry were multiplied. In time, as he had been forewarned, Paul would see how much he would suffer for the gospel's sake. Christians today also need ever to remember that the faithful proclamation of the gospel and the diligent pursuit of their world missions task will always be costly. They were never otherwise. The agony which the work of missions may at times require, however, is never to be compared to its ecstasy—the cost, with the reward.

21—Trails and Trials of the Early Missionary

Acts 20:4 to 21:40

The present chapter unfolds some of the most touching scenes recorded in Acts.

The Trial of Farewells

The third missionary journey of Paul was nearing its end. After a visit to certain parts of Greece (Acts 20:2-3), Paul concluded this tour and began a long return trip to Jerusalem.

We learn from his second letter to Corinth (2 Cor. 8 and 9) that the apostle had been gathering funds for the aid of needy Christians in Jerusalem. The time had come to deliver these. Accompanying him on the journey were several men from Berea, Thessalonica, and other places.

Paul wanted to get back to Jerusalem by Pentecost (Acts 20:16). Yet there were certain points at which he desired one more visit with the brethren. One of these was Philippi. Although Acts only mentions departure from this city, it must have been with profound joy that the brethren there were privileged once more to see the beloved missionary.

We are told more clearly of a service Paul later held in Troas. This city will be remembered as the place where he had received the vision calling him to Europe (Acts 16:8-9). A church had been formed at Troas. The congregation met with the apostle and his companions in a service which was to last all night. The service was held "upon the first day of the week" (Acts 20:7). This is the first recorded instance that Christians had now begun to worship on Sunday instead of Saturday.

A young man, by the name of Eutychus (Acts 20:9), having fallen asleep, fell from a window on the third floor where the service was held and was thought to be dead. Luke, as a physician, was especially impressed with the story that Paul was able to restore Eutychus to the congregation. What Paul declared on that memorable evening is not recounted.

Luke may not have been present at Troas, but he later went with the group to Assos (Acts 20:13). The modest statement, "we went before," is Luke's way of including himself. It is striking that Paul chose to let his party go on by ship while he himself went by foot. Why he walked the twenty miles or so between Troas and Assos is not told. Was it because he simply wanted to be alone? The trial of saying good-by to congregations he loved and the thought of not seeing them again must have weighed heavily upon him. Paul boarded the ship at Assos and sailed to Miletus with the others.

The Momentous Meeting at Miletus

Upon Paul's arrival at Miletus, he sent to Ephesus and called the elders to meet him for a conference. The distance and mode of travel then would have required at least three days for these elders to be notified and to get to Miletus. Why Paul did not go to Ephesus is not mentioned.

A rather large group readily responded to the apostle's invitation. Their meeting with him forms one of the most tender moments in the whole ministry of the apostle. He was fully aware that this would be his last meeting with them. Hence his farewell message deserves all the more to be examined carefully. He related here certain things not mentioned elsewhere either in Acts or in his Epistles. One of these was that the Holy Spirit had already given him evidence "in every city" that bonds and afflictions lay ahead of him (Acts 20:23). Nowhere was his complete dedication and personal heroism more clearly in view than in his declaration: "But none of these things move me, neither count I my life dear unto myself, so that I might finish my course with joy, and the ministry, which I have received of the Lord Jesus, to testify the gospel of the grace of God" (Acts 20:24).

Paul affirmed he had not shunned a declaration of the full counsel of God. He warned of wolves that would enter into the flock and cause division and distress. He foresaw that even some of those present would themselves cause disunity. Apprehensions such as these must have pained him deeply.

One of the heartaches of any true missionary is likely his uneasiness about what may happen to the work God has wrought through him after his departure. There is always a possibility that problems and dissensions may undo much of what has been accomplished.

The church of Ephesus mentioned in Revelation 2:1-7 is the same one Paul addresses now. It is consoling to know that this church took Paul's warning seriously. It evidently concerned itself notably in later years with warding off divisions and erroneous teaching in its midst.

Paul disclosed to the Ephesian brethren that he felt bound in the Spirit to go to Jerusalem despite what lay ahead of him. We are not told what gave him this sense of compulsion. We can only suppose that it was more than a mere desire to deliver the offering he had gathered. The Holy Spirit both forewarned him of the cost of his going to Jerusalem and pressed him with the necessity of the journey.

Paul recounted to the Ephesians how he had taken care of his own support while in their midst. He had not depended upon them for anything but for prayer and love. In connection with this discussion he recalled a statement of Christ which otherwise has no record in the New Testament: "It is more blessed to give than to receive" (Acts 20:35). Paul discovered that a life of self-giving service to others is a life of highest satisfaction. That he thought it wise to support himself by his own labors is not to be taken as an argument that missionaries should not be supported now. Indeed, Paul more than once emphasized that a workman is worthy of his hire. He believed churches should support their ministers and missionaries.

In the pioneer areas in which he ministered, of course, his work might have been misunderstood had he not sustained himself. He had no denomination or mission board back of him. It is, therefore, all the more to his honor that he went anyway. Such heroism in no whit, however, relieves Christians today of a grave responsibility to support with prayer and money those whom they send out.

After Paul had concluded his farewell address to the brethren from Ephesus, he knelt down with them. They all prayed together. What a tender and holy scene that was! The brethren wept, "sorrowing most of all for the words which he spake, that they should see his face no more" (Acts 20:38).

The Final Journey to Jerusalem

Luke detailed the course not only from Greece to Miletus (Acts 20:14-15) but also from Miletus to Caesarea Philippi. The cities and places named such as Coos, Rhodes, Patara, and Phoenicia were all of great historical significance. Coos, for example, was the home of Hippocrates, whose famous oath for doctors has so affected medical history. At Rhodes had stood one of the wonders of the ancient world, the celebrated Colossus. Paul would have been aware, as would Luke, of the fame of each place mentioned. His interest, though, concerned something of greater importance—the spreading of the gospel to all the world.

Paul's ship finally reached Tyre, a city mentioned in the Old Testament, the center of Phoenician maritime power. There was now a congregation of Christians in this city also. These met Paul during the stopover. The missionary and his group remained for seven days (Acts 21:4). Here, too, Paul received further warnings against the dangers that lay before him. So dear to the congregation was this valiant missionary and teacher, that not only the elders, but also the women and children followed him to the ship and knelt on shore with him in prayer as he departed. They, too, likely bade him a tearful farewell.

Sailing to Ptolemais, Paul disembarked and went by land to Caesarea. Here in the home of Philip the evangelist, the daughters of Philip, in whom there was a spirit of prophecy, warned Paul. Also Agabus, who came down from Judea, vividly declared the dangers which lay before the apostle in Jerusalem (Acts 21:8-11).

Luke was still in the company. He said, "And when we heard these things, both we, and they of that place, besought him not to go up to Jerusalem" (Acts 21:12). The Christians in Caesarea were fully aware of the hostility toward Paul which now pervaded Jerusalem. Paul's own companions were also convinced he ought not to go on. Their entreaties were earnest and extended. Paul responded, "What mean ye to weep and to break mine heart?" (Acts 21:13). He again affirmed his purpose by saying, "I am ready not to be bound only, but also to die at Jerusalem for the name of the Lord Jesus." Seeing that they could not discourage him, they ceased to try. Their resigned response was, "The will of the Lord be done" (Acts 21:14).

When Paul and his company reached Jerusalem, the brethren there received them gladly. The following day the leaders of the church, including James, came together. Paul recited "what things God had wrought among the Gentiles by his ministry" (Acts 21:19). These at Jerusalem were moved to glorify God. They reported how many thousands of Jews in Judea had also become believers. The inference is that Jerusalem and all of Judea were now covered with professing Christians. This very fact, as significant as it was, also posed a problem. That problem was the prejudice which yet lingered among these Jewish Christians toward Gentile believers. Their growing numbers also intensified the hostility of unconverted Jews. The atmosphere was tense. James, therefore, recommended that Paul observe certain Jewish religious ceremonials in the Temple (Acts 21:23-25) as evidence that he had not taught others to forsake the Law of Moses.

Paul was thus confronted with a crisis. He had long since been convinced that in God's sight there was no Jew or Gentile, and that believers are one in Christ. Paul was persuaded, though, to go through the rite recommended, and was in the process of doing so when an explosive event took place. On the last day of the ceremonial, he was recognized by Jews from Ephesus. These Jews had earlier seen him in the city with Trophimus from Ephesus and had assumed that Paul had brought this Gentile into the Temple. They suddenly raised a cry against Paul. This set off mob reaction. Soon Paul was bound in the same city where, years ago, he himself had bound Christians for professing the name he now considered above every name.

In a later study we shall review Paul's witness which was given before both Jewish and Gentile rulers.

The trials of Paul had led him in the years since his conversion throughout the greater part of the Roman Empire with the gospel. He could write to the church at Corinth, "In journeyings often, in perils of waters, in perils of robbers, in perils by mine own countrymen, in perils by the heathen, in perils in the city, in perils in the wilderness, in perils in the sea, in perils among false brethren" (2 Cor. 11:26). His course was to be exhausting and costly.

The history of missions has often fortunately been the story of triumphs and joys. It has also been a story of trials and tears. The latter seems an inevitable price that some must pay if the gospel is to be successfully spread in the earth. Paul gladly paid the price.

22—Missionary Witness to Rulers and Nations

Acts 22:1 to 26:32

If the gospel is to reach all men, it must somehow reach leaders and rulers of nations as well as others.

Dr. Billy Graham has been privileged to preach to presidents, kings, and other heads of state in many parts of the world. Many of our denominational leaders and missionaries have sought repeatedly to convey the terms of the gospel to government officials in various lands. Dr. R. G. Lee has told of his experience in bearing witness to the late Mr. Jawaharlal Nehru, prime minister of India.

It was inevitable that Paul, the great missionary, would in time proclaim the gospel, if he could do so, even to Caesar himself. Paul longed to see followers of Judaism as well as of heathen religions come to Christ. Whether or not he foresaw an opportunity in his last visit to the Holy City to proclaim the gospel to the leaders of the Jews as well as in Gentile courts, such was the case.

When Paul had been rescued from the mob which sought to kill him in the Temple, his response was to appeal to the officer in charge to permit him to speak. In the spirit of Christ, he addressed those who had wanted to kill him as "men, brethren, and fathers" (Acts 22:1). He proudly and positively professed his indebtedness to the Jewish faith, mentioning that he had studied in Jerusalem at the feet of the famed Gamaliel. He had not only been careful to follow the way of his fathers; he had also sought to root out all heresy. In pursuit of this purpose, he had persecuted followers of Christ "unto the death." With authorization from the high priest, he had proceeded to Damascus to blot out this sect there. Coming to his main point, he told of how his whole life had been changed on the road to Damascus. He had heard the voice of Christ speak to him and had seen a light he could not forget. Paul related how he was blinded until Ananias was sent with directions which were to be Paul's orders for the remainder of his life. His commission involved bearing the gospel to the Gentiles.

When the throng heard the word "Gentiles" it was like the touching of a switch setting off an explosion. Ripping off their clothing and throwing dust into the air, the crowd rushed on him with frenzy. The captain, not knowing Paul was a Roman citizen, started to have the apostle beaten. Paul then informed him of his Roman citizenship and was delivered from the beating.

The captain, however, decided that on the morrow he would bring Paul before the Jewish Sanhedrin to see what their charges were. This led to Paul's personal encounter with the leaders of the Jews, an encounter which was to be decisive and revealing. Undoubtedly knowing these leaders to be informed concerning his past, Paul came to the heart of his message, the proclamation of the resurrection.

Mention of the resurrection divided the camp. Paul, of course, had been convinced by his vision of the living Christ that Jesus was risen, indeed risen from the dead.

The above events afforded the apostle opportunity to pursue his missionary purpose, the proclaiming of Jesus in the very Temple courts and to the rulers of his own nation. His concern was not a mere defense of himself. In writing to the Romans later, Paul would say that he wished himself a castaway if by so being Israel could be saved.

An interesting personal glimpse into the life of the apostle here occurs. Paul's nephew somehow learned that certain Jews had banded themselves together not to eat or sleep until they could kill Paul. Their scheme was to have Paul brought down the next day before the council and to slay him on the way. Mention of Paul's sister's son reveals that at least some of Paul's family now lived in Jerusalem. Their interest in his protection suggests also that Paul's sister and possibly her family were among the believers in the city. Paul would be as concerned to reach his family as to reach others. The true missionary is burdened for his loved ones as well as for the world.

The night before the council was to meet, Paul had a special vision which probably was a comfort to him through all the difficult years ahead. In that vision, according to Luke, "the Lord stood by him, and said, Be of good cheer, Paul: for as thou hast testified of me in Jerusalem, so must thou bear witness also at Rome" (Acts 23:11).

The report of Paul's sister's son was given to the chief captain who made immediate plans to deliver Paul to the Roman governor at Caesarea. With a special bodyguard of nearly five hundred soldiers the apostle was sent out of the city, departing from it for the last time. It must have been a consolation to recall later that he had not let this last opportunity to preach Christ there go by the board. At the risk of death, he made every possible effort to call the leaders of the Jews and all others who heard him to belief in Christ.

Paul was to be a prisoner in Caesarea for more than two years. During this time, he would proclaim the same gospel to the Roman governors, Felix and Festus, and even to King Agrippa!

Five days after Paul was taken to Caesarea, Felix gave his case a hearing. Tertullus, representing the high priest and elders, charged that Paul was a disturber of the peace, a revolutionist, a representative of a sect not permitted by Roman law, and a desecrater of the Temple. The charges were so untrue that Paul had only to appeal for proof of them to demonstrate their falsity. Correcting the account about his presence in the Temple, he moved on to interpret the faith he professed and to state the real reason (Acts 24:17) he had been in Jerusalem. He then spoke of the resurrection, a major note in apostolic preaching.

Later when Lysias, the chief captain in Jerusalem, came down to Caesarea, Felix gave Paul another hearing. As Paul "reasoned of righteousness, temperance, and judgment to come, Felix trembled, and answered, Go thy way for this time; when I have a convenient season, I will call for thee" (Acts 24:25).

Felix, through his Jewish wife, already knew much about Jewish teaching. Against this background, Paul pressed home the claims of Christ upon the life of this Roman official.

Although Felix trembled under the impact of the gospel, he adopted a tactic so often used by those who, though convicted of their own guilt and need, refuse to turn from their evil way. He postponed a decision. Luke says Felix also hoped to receive a bribe for releasing Paul.

Festus, who succeeded Felix, on visiting Jerusalem, was reminded of Paul by the Jews who still wished to see him killed. Festus suggested they come down to Caesarea for a hearing (Acts 25:7).

Motivated more by a desire to please the Jews than to give Paul justice, Festus asked Paul if he were willing to go back to Jerusalem to be judged there. At this point the apostle appealed to Caesar.

Because Festus had no charge against Paul, he welcomed an opportunity to have King Agrippa hear Paul also. Agrippa was partly Jew and more informed than either Felix or Festus concerning Jewish beliefs. He was accompanied by his sister who was living incestuously with him as his wife at the time. With great pomp, preparations were made for the hearing of Paul. Far from being a prisoner at the bar, however, Paul used the occasion not as a defense of himself but as an opportunity to proclaim the gospel.

Accepting the fact that Agrippa knew a great deal about the customs and teachings of the Jews, Paul drove home the truth he felt called to proclaim. Recounting his own personal experience both in the days he persecuted Christians and in his conversion at Damascus, he then related how he had been called to preach the gospel to the Gentiles.

His mission was "to open their eyes, and to turn them from darkness to light, and from the power of Satan unto God, that they may receive forgiveness of sins, and inheritance among them which are sanctified by faith that is in me" (Acts 26:18). He then preached repentance. None needed this message more than Agrippa and Bernice! Paul referred to the prophetic promise of the coming of Christ and the fulfilment of that promise. His message was so powerful that it moved Festus to cry out, "Paul, thou art beside thyself; much learning doth make thee mad" (Acts 26:24).

However, Paul pressed on for a verdict. Addressing the king personally, he asked, "King Agrippa, believest thou the prophets? I know that thou believest" (Acts 26:27). This moved Agrippa to reply, "Almost thou persuadest me to be a Christian" (Acts 26:28).

One of the greatest sermons ever preached, Paul's message to this Roman court lives on. It truly exalted Christ.

The record indicates Herod was convinced of the innocence of Paul, as was Festus; and if Paul had not appealed to Rome, he could have been set free. Was Paul sorry for his appeal to Caesar? There is no indication of it. Having preached before governors and kings of the empire, he would now possibly even be able to proclaim the gospel to Caesar himself!

23—Missionaries in an Inhospitable World

Acts 27:1 to 28:31

Missions and Crises

"This topsy-turvy world," said Dr. Baker J. Cauthen, "is like a ship in a rough sea: it continues to roll and toss. As soon as a crisis passes in one place, another develops elsewhere." These crises have their inevitable effect, as Dr. Cauthen further notes, upon the work of missions as they do on many other areas of life. The history of missions has always been interwoven with crises. Often obstacles and trials have risen before the missionary. Yet, despite these, he has marched from one victory to another.

"Missions is a part of the genius of Christianity," insists Earl R. Cook. "Broadly conceived," he adds, "it is the deliberate attempt to bring to others the blessings of the Christian faith, whether at home or abroad," That deliberate attempt, however, has taken missions and missionaries through many a testing time, both by land and by sea. Paul's experience often revealed how perilous these tests could be and yet how profitable to the missionary witness.

Paul, Bound for Rome

The pomp and splendor of the Roman court in Caesarea has long since faded into dust. The great sermon Paul preached there before Agrippa, Bernice, and Festus, however, lives on. History discloses that, although Herod and Festus left Paul in chains to be delivered ultimately to Caesar in Rome, it was really they who were in bondage. His freedom in Christ and his consciousness that he had borne a faithful witness before both the rulers of his own people and the Roman rulers in Palestine enabled him to board ship for the capital city of the empire, not in defeat, but in triumph.

The account of Paul's journey to Rome, and especially the storm at sea (Acts 27), was masterfully and realistically portrayed by Luke. James Stalker says his journal of this voyage is the most valuable document concerning the seamanship of ancient times that remains in existence. We perhaps owe this to the fact that Luke appears to have been with Paul on the journey and thus to have shared the experience. To him it was unforgettable.

The details of the trip to Rome need not here be recounted. It is important, however, to note that the prisoner on board became in the hour of peril virtually the master of the ship. His heaven-sent wisdom, towering faith, and confidence that the Lord would let him see Rome, a confidence based on a revelation from God (Acts 27:23-25), left him untouched by fear even when hardened sailors lost hope. Indeed, aboard ship he became the one around whom soldiers and sailors were able to gather. Prisoner though he was, the life of every man aboard was in his hands. Still the great, heroic missionary, he gave witness by life as well as by word to God whom he served.

Neither Acts nor tradition tells us whether anyone aboard was led to faith in Christ through Paul's testimony. One cannot help but wonder, however, how many a salty seaman or toughened soldier may have lived to remember that frail missionary who stood so tall among them in this terrifying experience and, remembering, may have given a more attentive ear to the gospel soon heralded across the empire.

Shipwrecked in Melita

Acts is notably brief in its description of the three months during which Paul and apparently all who were aboard were marooned in Melita (Malta) after the shipwreck. Luke's attention seems to have been centered almost exclusively on things of special interest to a physician. He noted Paul's laying of hands upon the father of Publius, praying for him, and healing him. He noted the effect of this healing upon the natives and how they were moved by it to bring the diseased to Paul for help. Some have wondered whether Luke also, as a physician, may have joined Paul in this ministry which could be classified now as medical missions. That what was done made a great impression upon the people of Malta is obvious. Strangely, however, we are not told that Paul preached the gospel to them or that any were won to Christ. Again, is it too much to read between the lines that Luke may by now have expected his readers to conclude such was the case?

The natives at Malta are called in the Revised Standard Version "barbarians." This simply meant that they were people who did not speak Greek. Did Paul conclude that these less cultured people might understand a ministry to their physical needs better than his sermons? Whatever the case, it is reasonable to conclude, with Kraeling, "that the author of Acts thinks of this as the occasion of the founding of Christianity on Malta." We can be certain that Paul would, under every circumstance, have continued to be a faithful missionary.

Here, as aboard ship, to use the language of Dr. Frank Stagg, "though still a prisoner, [Paul] manifested pre-eminence. On board ship he was still the biggest man among them." He was also in Malta the biggest man among them.

As soon as weather permitted, the officer who had Paul in custody arranged for ship to Rome. Arriving at Puteoli, the main harbor of Italy, located some 135 miles from Rome, Paul found a company of Christians already in this port city. The centurion surprisingly permitted Paul to spend seven days with these believers. Then came the march to Rome.

The Appian Way, over which Paul passed, was now famous. Many a place of historical significance as well as the estates of some of the most wealthy and famous people of the empire lay along it. One of these estates was that of Cicero. Luke's attention, however, was not on such small details as these. It was on the advance of the great Christian warrior toward his ultimate objective. Dr. J. B. Lawrence is justified in referring to this experience as "after all a fourth missionary journey."

Long before, Paul had written to the church at Rome that he was ready with all that was within him to preach the gospel there also (Rom. 1:15). Though he was now moving toward this longed-for objective as a prisoner, he was nonetheless advancing with the courage of a conqueror. He bore in his bosom the message which he knew would set Rome and the whole empire free.

Through God's grace he would yet preach that liberating gospel to Caesar also!

Paul Met by a Delegation from Rome

At Appii Forum (Acts 28:15), forty-three miles from Rome, Paul was met by a delegation from the capital city. Ten miles farther on, he was met by another group who had come out to welcome him. During the two years of Paul's imprisonment at Caesarea, many travelers had perhaps brought news about Paul from that city to Rome. They would have been sure to stress Paul's professed innocence. Yet there were conflicting reports. It is to the credit of the Christians in Rome that, disregarding Paul's being a prisoner, they went to such effort to greet him. When Paul saw these friends, he thanked God and took courage. The spirit of this valiant missionary had apparently begun now to quaver. This is understandable. He was worn from his labors and was suffering the humiliation of his chains. Had he begun to wonder also whether he would be equal to his opportunity? Whatever feeling of depression may have temporarily come over him, his spirit was renewed and his hope set ablaze by the coming of these friends. With firm and quickened step he marched toward the city before him. The presence with him of these two Christian groups brought him inspiration and warmed his heart.

As we recall the scene, it is easy also to catch a vision of thousands of other missionaries in all parts of the earth being greeted and welcomed by other small bands of native Christians, as they too move toward their destination of service.

Except for Paul's bonds, he could not have prayed for more than he was now experiencing. During the journey which would have taken at least two more days, Paul would surely have filled in all the gaps of information for the brethren from Rome, and more importantly, he would have recounted to them the wonders God had wrought through him and his fellow missionaries in all parts of the empire. How the group must have hung upon his words. Their excitement would have made them almost forget the bonds of the apostle.

Leniency was extended by the Roman authorities to Paul. Nero, now ruler of the empire, had perhaps allowed kinder officials than himself to handle Paul's case upon his arrival. Whatever the reason, Paul was given maximum liberty, being permitted to use his own rented house, and having only a Roman soldier as his guard.

Paul Wins Roman Officers

From Paul's letter to the Philippians, we learn that Paul was able to win at least some Roman officers to Christ. Not only was he having opportunity to preach to government officials, but he was doing so by their own arrangement!

Paul's rented house became a mecca at first for both Jew and Gentile. The Jews wanted to know more about the "sect" to which they heard Paul now belonged. Paul recounted to the Jews all that had transpired and why he had appealed to Caesar. Some of the Jews listened, as from morning until evening he proclaimed the gospel to them; and some believed. Paul felt moved to recall to others what Isaiah declared concerning the hardness of the heart of his own people (Acts 28:25-27). He then announced to the Jews: "Be it known therefore unto you, that the salvation of God is sent unto the Gentiles, and that they will hear it" (Acts 28:28). The judgment he expressed was not the cause of the Jews' rejection of Jesus but the result. That rejection led Paul to the further affirmation which seems to be basic in Acts: that Jewish rejection had opened the door for the proclamation of the gospel to the Gentiles.

The gospel had already reached Rome. Two or more congregations may already have existed in the city. These would have resulted from the testimony borne earlier by travelers. The work of these congregations would have been greatly strengthened and deepened by such marvelous documents as the book of Romans, which Paul had sometime before forwarded to them. Now the great missionary teacher was present himself!

Not only did Paul preach and teach every day, but he also found time to write some of his greatest masterpieces. Here, likely, as we shall later more particularly see, the apostle wrote such letters as Philemon, Ephesians, Colossians, and Philippians. The letter to Philemon resulted from the visit of a runaway slave from Colossae. The beautiful Philippian letter was prompted by a visit by Epaphroditus from Philippi, bringing a love offering. Questions about the nature of the church, its hope for the future, its ministry, and its mission prompted Paul, under the Spirit, to write the great epistle to the Ephesians, a book which has been called "the profoundest and the sublimest book in the world."

24—"This Is That . . ."

Acts

A glance back over the tremendous book of Acts is needed to summarize its immortal message. What is Acts all about? What particular message or messages does it especially underscore?

The book is called the Acts of the Apostles. It might as appropriately have been named the Acts of the Holy Spirit, or the Acts of Christ through the Holy Spirit. Jesus had promised: "But ye shall receive power, after that the Holy Ghost is come upon you: and ye shall be witnesses unto me both in Jerusalem, and in all Judea, and in Samaria, and unto the uttermost part of the earth" (Acts 1:8).

The phenomenon witnessed by the astonished multitudes at Pentecost was interpreted by Peter as being the fulfilment of Joel's prophecy: "But this is that which was spoken by the prophet Joel; and it shall come to pass in the last days, saith God, I will pour out of my Spirit upon all flesh: and your sons and your daughters shall prophesy, and your young men shall see visions, and your old men shall dream dreams: and on my servants and on my handmaidens I will pour out in those days of my Spirit; and they shall prophesy: and I will shew wonders in heaven above, and signs in the earth beneath; blood, and fire, and vapour of smoke. The sun shall be turned into darkness, and the moon into blood, before that great and notable day of the Lord come: and it shall come to pass, that whosoever shall call on the name of the Lord shall be saved" (Acts 2:16-21).

Here then was the beginning of the fulfilment of the Old Testament foreview of salvation history. "This is that . . ." The prophet, indeed, had predicted more perhaps than even Peter at the moment comprehended. "Whosoever shall call on the name of the Lord," he said, "shall be saved" (Acts 2:21).

The purpose of Luke seems to have been to disclose how the Christ, of whom he had already written in his Gospel, had been revealed unmistakably as the universal hope of humankind. Luke showed in Acts how the gospel advanced from Jerusalem to Judea, from Judea to Samaria, and from Samaria to the uttermost parts of the earth.

Indeed, five great universals stand out in Acts.

Universal Authority of the Holy Spirit

Throughout Acts, Luke seemed careful to disclose that every step which advanced the gospel in the world was governed and inspired by the Spirit. The Holy Spirit first filled the 120 in the Upper Room and enabled them to speak in languages understood by people from all over the empire. He guided the work of Philip among the Samaritans and with the Ethiopian enunch. Peter was convinced by the Spirit later that what he witnessed in the house of Cornelius was wrought by the same Holy Spirit who had been working among the Jews. He thus could not question the Spirit's authority.

The whole missionary enterprise of the church, from Antioch through Paul's three great missionary tours, was under the government of the Spirit. Paul felt himself subject always to the authority of the Spirit. The work of the Spirit, moreover, was evident not only among the various nations and races to whom the gospel was taken but also among every class and culture, whether barbarian or free, Greek or Roman, learned or unlearned. He could work in Jerusalem or Rome, Corinth or Athens, Antioch or Ephesus. He knew no boundary.

Universality of Human Need

By pointing out the many and varied groups represented at Pentecost, Luke appeared to say that all of these vast areas of the empire had the same needs as did citizens of Jerusalem. Their guilt had helped to nail Christ to the cross. For them God had raised up Jesus and given him a name above every other name. Indeed, there was "none other name under heaven" through which any man could be saved. Whether the paralytic at the gate of the Temple, the brilliant Saul of Tarsus, the Ethiopian official, Cornelius, the Philippian jailor, the citizens of cultured Athens or of corrupt Corinth—all were in need of the Saviour. From the cry of the throng in the streets of Jerusalem on the day of Pentecost ("Men and brethren, what shall we do?") to the petition of the jailor ("What must I do to be saved?"), all had needs so deep that only Christ could satisfy them.

Universal Relevance of the Gospel

It has been pointed out that the gospel is adequate for all the explosions of our present world—the population explosion with its attendant complexities, the explosion of knowledge, the explosion of rebellion, and all others which trouble men today. The gospel is the good news in our world.

It will not be forgotten that the book of Acts was written not by a Jew but by a converted Greek. Luke as a Gentile had found that the gospel was sufficient for him too. It was relevant for his day, his culture, and his world. He seemed confident that it would always be relevant.

Some ask today, Is the church relevant? The answer is that it is relevant as long as it bears the gospel of the good news of the saving grace of God.

In an issue of the *Bible Society Record,* Chaplain Major General Ivan L. Bennett referred to a visit to Seoul and to what he learned from one of the missionaries there. The missionary had acted as chaplain in a Korean prison camp. He reported to Chaplain Bennett that on a certain bulletin board at the theological seminary in Taegu, he had seen posted the names of 156 former prisoners captured with the Communist forces of North Korea. All, having completed their education at college and seminary, had since become ordained ministers and were at that time serving as ministers in the churches of Korea. The change which had taken place in these men resulted from the impact of the gospel.

As long as men are lost and in the bondage of sin, this gospel will remain the best news their ears have ever heard.

Universal Adequacy of the Risen Christ

Even the casual reader of Acts must be impressed by the burning conviction with which the early church proclaimed the fact of the resurrection. The resurrection reality had broken in on the disciples with convincing power. They had not at first believed it could be possible. Though Christ had repeatedly attempted to prepare them for both his death and resurrection, they apparently lost all hope as they saw him nailed to the cross. The sentiment among the disciples perhaps is reflected in the forlorn remark of one of them on the way to Emmaus on Easter morning. Said he to the Stranger who had joined him and his companion on the way, "But we trusted that it had been he which should have redeemed Israel: and beside all this, to day is the third day since these things were done" (Luke 24:21). What a phenomenal change took place after that hour! The forty days through which the risen Christ met repeatedly with the disciples awakened in them a burning conviction of his living presence. Hence, at Pentecost and thereafter, Christ was proclaimed as triumphant over the grave and as the Source and Author of life. In him alone could salvation be found. "Neither is there salvation in any other: for there is none other name under heaven given among men, whereby we must be saved" (Acts 4:12).

The effect of Jesus' saving power was as tremendous in Jerusalem on the day of Pentecost as the impact of an earthquake. On one day three thousand believed. Other thousands followed. Throughout Acts the story of changed men and women is recorded. Jew, Greek, Roman, Samaritan, Ethiopian—all found his salvation adequate. Even for Jews and others who later came to Paul's rented house in Rome, this same risen Saviour was powerful to redeem.

The example of good men has often become an inspiration to others for nobler living. Men of wisdom have frequently appeared, men whose teachings have enlightened others and enabled them to find a better life. But there has been only one who has triumphed over death and the grave, who has brought life and immortality to life, and who has been able to release men from sin and death, bringing them into the liberty of the sons of God. That man is the Lord Jesus Christ. This note Luke, the beloved physician and careful historian, seems exceedingly desirous to sound. He sounds the note on the basis of convincing evidence he had gathered in Palestine, Asia Minor, and Europe, and on the basis of his own observations. He apparently was especially desirous of stressing the sweeping significance of the appeal expressed by Paul to Agrippa: "I would to God, that not only thou, but also all that hear me this day, were both almost, and altogether such as I am, except these bonds" (Acts 26:29). Without the knowledge of which Paul was speaking even regal robes could not make a man free. With that knowledge neither chains nor prison could really enslave.

Universal Responsibility of the Church

Acts makes clear that every Christian is to be a witness, but this witness is not to be borne by human strength alone. The Holy Spirit will be with those who are obedient. His strength will make them sufficient. The support and the fellowship of other believers will also be a source of help. Beyond this, prayer of fellow believers will result in even the opening of prison doors.

Acts does not record the slightest evidence of any attempt to build a hierarchy over the churches or even to forge them into organizational unity. A deeper unity—a unity in Christ—was realized. Christian fellowship transcended all barriers, whether of race, nation, tongue, or culture. The touching scene Luke portrayed of the two bands of Christians which came out from Rome to meet Paul on his way from Puteoli gives living evidence of how Christians were then forged into a brotherhood which transcended every human barrier. That fellowship became a dynamic witness in a pagan world. Men began to realize, as they beheld how these followers of Christ loved one another, that something had happened to them which they themselves had not experienced. Christ's petition in the immortal prayer of John 17:21, "That they all may be one; as thou, Father, art in me, and I in thee, that they also may be one in us: that the world may believe that thou hast sent me," was being answered.

In all parts of the empire where the gospel had gone, Christians were bearing witness not only in their fellowship, in their love for one another, and the quality of life they now lived, but also by the testimony they bore in word. The most valiant witness portrayed in Acts, of course, is that of the apostle Paul on whom Luke chiefly focused his attention. With burning zeal the apostle sought to spread the gospel to all men. He stands out brilliantly, though not alone, as an example of the fulfilment of the abiding and universally binding commission of our Lord: "Ye shall be witnesses unto me both in Jerusalem, and in all Judea, and in Samaria, and unto the uttermost part of the earth" (Acts 1:8).

25—Missions in Pauline Messages

In the study of Acts, the heroic missionary zeal of Paul has been traced from his conversion to his imprisonment in Rome. The focus was on the activity of the apostle in preaching and teaching, both in Asia and in Europe. But attention was called at certain points to a part of Paul's work which Luke surprisingly failed to mention. This was the remarkable correspondence Paul carried on with churches in various parts of the empire.

Romans

Romans was addressed to Christians in the capital of the empire, where Paul had as yet never visited. Besides the weeks, or possibly months, required to write this epistle, there were dramatic aspects related to its transmission to Rome—probably by the hand of a prominent deaconess named Phoebe from Cenchrea near Corinth—which, it seems, would have attracted Luke's comment.

Written apparently from Corinth while Paul was vigorously engaged in missionary activity in that great commercial, corrupt city, Romans sets forth many of the doctrines basic to missions. The following easily attract attention:

The gospel is of universal power and relevance. Paul was not ashamed (was really proud) of the gospel, for he said, "It is the power of God unto salvation to every one that believeth" (Rom. 1:16), including Jew and Gentile. He felt under obligation both to Greeks and to barbarians, to the wise and the foolish, to preach that gospel wherever he could. His discovery of its power to transform his own life made him a debtor to share it with all.

The fallen condition of man, hence his need of redemption, is evident in man's history and experience. In a masterful telescoping of human experience, Paul disclosed how man has fallen into his present state and why the wrath of God thus rests upon him (Rom. 1:18 to 2:2). He emphasized that men are "without excuse" (Rom. 1:20), not having followed the revelation given to them and having refused to honor or give thanks to God. God, therefore, "gave them up," permitting them to explore the depths of their lusts and impurity of heart. The phrase "gave them up" runs like a horrifying refrain throughout the passage (Rom: 1:24,26,28).

The apostle returned to the argument stated in Rom. 1:20 as he began chapter 2: "Therefore you have no excuse, O man, whoever you are." Men's judging of one another and judging themselves by one another would have no effect on removing the judgment of God, for his judgment "rightly falls," the apostle insists, "upon those who do such things."

The impartiality of God leaves no exceptions or advantages for any man. Whether men have sinned without the law or under the law will in neither case justify them. Paul suggested in Romans 2:15 that some knowledge of what God desires men to be and do is written in men's hearts, whether they have received the revealed law of God or not. Both Gentile and Jew, even if the Jews adhere to such religious rites as circumcision, are sinners. Only religious rites which first arise out of a changed heart are of any meaning (Rom. 2:29). Any advantage the Jew has is solely that of a greater knowledge of the will of God. But knowing better, he becomes even more guilty. "What then? are we Jews any better off?" he asked. "No, not at all; for I have already charged that all men, both Jews and Greeks, are under the power of sin" (Rom. 3:9). There is, therefore, no distinction nor partiality with God (Rom. 3:22). All have sinned and fallen short of the glory of God and are thereby equally in need of redemption through the blood of Christ.

It is impossible for man to save himself. No amount of "works" can effect redemption. Not even an Abraham, who stood at the head of his race and sought faithfully to do the will of God, was saved by works. His works instead grew out of his faith.

The grace of God, made effective through Christ, is an adequate remedy for all sin. Christ died for helpless and ungodly men (Rom. 5:6). Through his death and resurrection every ungodly soul may be brought into reconciliation with God.

It seems clear from Romans 5:12-14 that Paul understood all men to be under the same condemnation and equally in need of

Christ. All who believe on him may be freed from the power of sin and brought into justification. "For the wages of sin is death (obviously for every man), but the free gift of God is eternal life in Christ Jesus our Lord," (obviously, too, the hope of everyone who seeks it). Paul could, therefore, rejoice confidently in the assurance that "There is therefore now no condemnation to them which are in Christ Jesus" (Rom. 8:1).

Fellowship, or oneness in Christ, transcends all earthly barriers. This point is suggested in the last chapter of Romans where Paul referred, not only to Phoebe, but also to many at Rome who represented various nations, cultural backgrounds, races, and areas. All were now made one in Christ.

Paul's compassion for his fellow Jews filled him with a missionary compulsion to win them too to Christ. In the opening of chapter 9 Paul affirmed he had great sorrow and unceasing anguish of heart for his brethren. His concern was so deep he even wished himself "cut off from Christ" if by this his people could be brought to salvation. He affirmed again in Romans 10:1, "My heart's desire and prayer to God for them (Israel) is that they may be saved." He bore in his heart, like a pain that would never leave him, a burden to see his fellow Jews know the salvation offered them through Christ.

1 and 2 Corinthians

First and Second Corinthians are thought by many to have been the most significant of the apostle's letters. In them the true character of the great missionary stands forth vividly. His definition of the gospel and his awareness that the church must be as Christ taught are also included in these letters.

First Corinthians was written at Ephesus, probably two or three years earlier than Romans, and sent across the Aegean Sea to Corinth. In this great epistle, a number of emphases vital to the work of missions stand forth:

In Christ crucified both the wisdom and the power of God are made effectual for all who believe. As Luke's account in Acts (16; 18; 19:1-20) disclosed, Paul had preached the gospel in Athens, famous for its philosophers, before he went to Corinth. He knew the philosophies of that day, even as he knew the inadequacies of Hebrew legalism. "Where is the wise man?" he reasoned, and declared God has made foolish "the wisdom of the world." The world by its wisdom had never found or known God.

In the same epistle, Paul later defined the gospel as, in essence, "That Christ died for our sins according to the scriptures; and that he was buried, and that he rose again the third day according to the scripture" (1 Cor. 15:3-4). This central truth is the source of the good news, and thus of the wisdom and power of God, disclosed in Christ. The gospel is *the* good news for *all* men.

Glimmers of the gospel had appeared early in human experience, possibly as early as in the promises of God to Adam, and certainly as early as in his promises to Abraham. Isaiah, however, apparently was the first to use the phrase "good tidings" (Isa. 40:1-9), which in the New Testament became "gospel." In Isaiah, the glorious significance of these good tidings was revealed to be God's redemptive purpose effected through his Servant, the Messiah. That purpose, even as Isaiah saw, was to be worldwide in its reach, embracing every nation and race. This gospel Paul preached, with the certainty that it was *the* answer to human need and hopelessness everywhere.

As in Romans, Paul again in 1 Corinthians emphasized that as "in Adam all die, so also in Christ shall all be made alive" (1 Cor. 15:22). In this context a fuller statement is given than in Romans concerning the certainty of resurrection and of the triumph of believers over the power of death. No other religion, then or now, offers a saviour who himself has "swallowed up death in victory" and is thus able to deliver those who trust in him from the bondage of death.

Paul underscored again the certainty of the universal reign of Christ (1 Cor. 15:24-28). Even death itself is to be brought under his dominion! This last enemy of man is by the cross "destroyed." Indeed, Paul insisted that "He must reign, till he hath put all enemies under his feet" (1 Cor. 15:25). The same theme is emphasized elsewhere, even under more trying conditions for the apostle, as in his prison letter to the Philippians.

Paul instructed Corinthians in practical issues of the Christian life. The church at Corinth was by no means perfect. Immorality and paganism dominated the culture of Corinth. Thus the city was a testing ground, in the fullest sense, for those who had become followers of Christ. The tests and temptations they faced led Paul, through the Spirit, to set down principles as valid even for today as they were then!

Second Corinthians, which from references in the letter may

be judged to have actually been the third, or possibly the fourth, letter he wrote Corinth, is distinctive for its autobiographical material. It comes as near disclosing the secret of Paul's own commitment to Christ and his victorious service as do all his other letters combined. The epistle reveals that the brave effort of the apostle, both in person and by letter, had a wholesome effect on the church at Corinth. Paul was greatly comforted and reassured by the response of the church, especially to his written instructions. The response affords a confirmation of the apostle's belief that a life transformed by Christ may become victorious over an evil society about it and be effective in transforming that society.

Galatians

This epistle, called by some "The Magna Charta of Christian liberty," deals directly and vigorously with a doctrine basic to Christian faith and hence to missions. The doctrine is that justification comes through faith alone. The Galatian Christians were being told that to be saved one must submit to Jewish ritual as well as believe in Christ. Paul insisted that if "justification were through the law, then Christ died to no purpose." He made his case for salvation through faith and not through works so strong that some have mistakenly concluded James and he contradicted each other. The apostle, however, was speaking of how men *become* Christians; James spoke of the kind of life consistent with Christian profession.

Paul reasoned that everyone, when judged by the law, has sinned but that all, whether Jew or Gentile, slave or free, male or female, are made sons of God through faith in Christ (Gal. 3:26). "Stand fast therefore in the liberty wherewith Christ hath made us free, and be not entangled again with the yoke of bondage" (Gal. 5:1).

Ephesians

One of the several letters written by Paul while imprisoned in Rome, Ephesians, was considered by many to have been the most sublime he ever wrote. Lacking the personal greetings characteristic of Paul's other letters, Ephesians is thought to have been a kind of circular letter addressed to the churches. It may have been identified with Ephesus because the copy finally used in the formation of the New Testament canon might have been preserved by and obtained from that church. Whether it is a general letter or not, it has abiding value for the whole body of Christ. Every local congregation, as well as the church as a whole, will find in it a treasure house of inspiration and guidance. Its meaning for missions is timeless and tremendous. It stresses:

The universal lordship of Christ. In the great prayer of the first chapter (Eph. 1:15-23), Paul reveals his unceasing petition that Christians everywhere be enlightened concerning the hope to which Christ has called them, the riches of Christ's inheritance in the saints and the "immeasurable greatness" of God's power available to those who believe. Christ, raised from the dead and seated at the right hand of the Father, above all rule and authority, power and dominion, bears a name above every name. All things are placed under his feet, and he is made head over all. This supremacy is amazingly stated as "to the church, which is his body, the fulness of him that filleth all in all" (Eph. 1:22-23).

The revelation of the place of the church in the plan of God. The passage just noted and Ephesians 2:19-22 and 5:23-27 provide a definition and description of the church, revealing that it is the body, the building, and the bride of Christ; a colony of heaven on earth; and the very household and temple of God. There is an inference, moreover, in Ephesians 6:10-17 that it is the army of the Lord, especially prepared not only to resist but to bring evil powers to a standstill. The scope of its task, therefore, is global and of eternal consequence.

The transforming power of the crucified and risen Christ to change all men. Whether the walls which separate men are national, racial, social, or cultural, Christ, in the view of the epistle, can make of the "twain" one.

In our world of growing alienation Christ is the one adequate reconciling power available. He not only enables the alienated to be reconciled, despite barriers that separate them, but removes these barriers: "For he is our peace, who hath made both one, and hath broken down the middle wall of partition between us; having abolished in his flesh the enmity, even the law of commandments contained in ordinances; for to make in himself of twain one new man, so making peace; and that he might reconcile both unto God in one body by the cross, having slain the enmity thereby" (Eph. 2:14-16).

Not only did the apostle in Ephesians outline some of the highest objectives and truths related to missions but he also dealt practically with the personal, marriage, vocational, and social relationships of Christians which affect their witness (Eph. 1:1 to 6:9). In the magnificent doxology at the end of chapter 3 he prayed that glory might come to Christ through the church. He proceeded in chapter 4 with the petition that Christians, therefore, lead a life worthy of the vocation to which they are called.

Philippians

This beautiful epistle could well be called a missionary's love letter to a church. Paul apparently wrote it while he was a prisoner in Rome, though its joyous tone has caused some to wonder whether the letter could have come out of a prison cell. Some points in it, especially related to missions, are:

The church at Philippi was an exemplary product of missionary work in an unpromising field. Though Paul had felt called to Macedonia (Acts 16:6-11), he had hardly begun his work there when hostility led to severe punishment of himself and Titus and their being fastened in the stocks of the inner prison. But out of this beginning came a church of such generosity, influence, and Christian commitment, that the very thought of it brought joy to the apostle's heart. He could, therefore, say, "I thank God upon every remembrance of you" (Phil. 1:3).

Paul was concerned to reassure this church (which loved him enough to send him financial support while he was a prisoner) that his present circumstances had turned out in truth to be a blessing in disguise. They offered him an unusual and almost unbelievable opportunity for preaching the gospel in the very halls of the Roman government (Phil. 1:12-14). Roman officers in contact with Paul heard of Christ. At least some in turn took the message to others. The result was that many even in "Caesar's household" were converted. This is evidence that the gospel, when proclaimed by a committed Christian, has power to penetrate even the strongest barriers.

Paul affirmed the humiliation and the exaltation of Christ. Likely having in mind the Messianic promise in Isaiah (45:23), Paul spoke of Christ's incomparable emptying of himself. Though having the form of God, he stooped to take on himself not only the form of man but also of a servant, becoming obedient even to the death of the cross. God, therefore, highly exalted him and gave him a name that is above every name, "That at the name of Jesus every knee should bow, of things in heaven, and things in earth, and things under the earth; and that every tongue should confess that Jesus Christ is Lord, to the glory of God the Father" (Phil. 2:5-11). What the people had foreseen, the apostle beheld in process of realization and, beholding it, was inspired to foresee also its climax in history. This hope is one of the solid rocks on which the work of Christian missions stands.

Colossians

Though shorter than Ephesians and Philippians, Colossians is packed with truth related to missions. The epistle, after a beautiful salutation, notes the progress being made at Colossae and rejoices in it: "The gospel which has come to you, as indeed in the whole world it is bearing fruit and growing—so among yourselves . . ." Though Paul was in prison, yet the gospel was still being preached both by himself and others and was being scattered to the ends of the empire. He saw it bearing fruit in the whole world and growing in its impact.

A further declaration in this epistle of highest missionary significance is its emphasis on the cosmic Christ (Col. 1:15-20; 2:9). Though somewhat similar to other statements by the apostle, Paul's comment here on the universal dominion of Christ merits special study. Christ is called the "first born" from the dead (Col. 1:15). For him and through him all creation came into being. In him the fullness of God dwells, and through him God will reconcile all things to himself.

Inferred, if not definitely declared in Colossians 1:27, is the global mission of the Christian witness. To the saints, as to Paul was given the privilege to see "the riches of the glory of this mystery among the Gentiles; which is Christ in you, the hope of glory" (Col. 1:27).

The epistle contains, moreover, an always relevant warning against false philosophies and traditions that lead only to dead ends. Paul warned the Colossians: "Beware lest any man spoil you through philosophy and vain deceit, after the tradition of men, after the rudiments of the world, and not after Christ" (Col. 2:8). On the cross Christ discarded the evil powers and authorities of this world like a garment; he made a public spectacle of them and led them as captives in his triumphal procession (Col. 2:15).

As in Ephesians, Paul in Colossians not only gave expression to doctrines basic to Christian faith as a whole and thus to missions, but again set out in simple and practical terms the kind of life which must properly grow out of one's having been "raised with Christ" (Col. 3:1-46). Guidelines are laid down, which if taken to heart everywhere, would change the world.

1 and 2 Thessalonians

Probably the first letters written by Paul still in existence, these two addressed to the church at Thessalonica are significant not so much for what they say about missions as for what they imply.

Paul had gone to Thessalonica shortly after his work in Philippi (Acts 17:1). His stay there was brief, but it was long enough for a vigorous church to be founded. The church though was in need of greater maturity both in knowledge and in Christian experience. Yet Paul had cause to boast of it. Its work of faith, labor of love, steadfastness of hope (1 Thess. 2:3), growing faith and mutual love justified it (2 Thess. 1:2,31). To be able to say as much about any church would be a high commendation.

This church, however, was under persecution and needed encouragement. Perplexing questions had also been raised about the second advent of Christ and what would be the state of those who were not living at the time of his appearance. To answer these questions and to strengthen members of the church, Paul gave simple but comprehensive explanations. He then dealt with some of the weaknesses there which, if continued, would handicap the church's witness as a missionary congregation. One of these was a tendency toward idleness, or being, as Paul said, "busy bodies" (2 Thess. 3:11), and not attending faithfully and soberly to their own tasks. To be personally responsible and never to become weary in well doing were vital to their influence in the world.

Though not dealing directly with missionary themes, these epistles were designed to develop a missionary-minded, exemplary church whose influence would grow and whose witness would have a very great effect on unbelievers.

1 and 2 Timothy and Titus

First and Second Timothy and Titus relate to the missionary message of the Bible largely in their explanation of the kind of persons church leaders ought to be. In these epistles, too, the organization and structures of the churches resulting from missionary labors are disclosed.

Though Pauline authorship of these epistles is often called in question there is much in them which seems fully in keeping with the great missionary's concern. Local congregations or churches depend for their influence and Christian service on the quality of their leadership. It is possible, as Paul said (1 Tim. 1:19), for some to make shipwreck of the faith by their own neglect. To Timothy and to all who confess Christ the instruction is given "Fight the good fight" (1 Tim. 6:12). Paul added "Do good . . . (and) be rich in good works" (1 Tim. 6:18).

The apostle declared, "For the time will come when they will not endure sound doctrine; but after their own lusts shall they heap to themselves teachers, having itching ears; and they shall turn away their ears from the truth, and shall be turned unto fables. But watch thou in all things, endure afflictions, do the work of an evangelist, make full proof of thy ministry" (2 Tim. 4:5). To do the work of an evangelist and truly to fulfill one's ministry is God's purpose for everyone called to missionary service and thus for every Christian.

Careful study of the Pastoral Epistles, as well as others Paul wrote, concerning the kind of life professing Christians ought to live, is urgently needed.

Philemon

This short letter, written also while Paul was under house arrest in Rome (Acts 28:30), is a revealing evidence of the transforming power of the gospel. Addressed to Philemon, a man of evident prominence and affluence, it concerns a runaway slave who had somehow found Paul and had been led to Christ by him. A changed man now, he was sent back by the apostle to his master, perhaps to serve him as never before, yet no longer as a slave but as a brother! Such a statement as this sounded the death knell of slavery and revealed at the same time the nature and power of Christian brotherhood.

26—Missions in Hebrews, the General Epistles, and Revelation

Hebrews

Though its missionary message may at first seem hidden, this book is possibly the greatest missionary treatise in the New Testament. It begins with the affirmation that God has been speaking to men across the centuries through those chosen for the purpose. He now, however, speaks through his Son. This Son is owner of all things, the one through whom the world and the universe were created, the "express image of God." Those who reject him and turn away from his grace have no other hope. Through this Christ, men enter into the kingdom eternal. "Therefore let us be grateful for receiving a kingdom that cannot be shaken," Hebrews pleads, "and thus let us offer to God acceptable worship, with reverence and awe; for our God is a consuming fire" (Heb. 12:28-29).

James

This letter deals indirectly with the missionary task. It seems to echo much of what is found in the Sermon on the Mount, which James may personally have heard. James' purpose was to guide Christians in the kind of living that would be a true expression of what Christ taught and thus a convincing witness in the world. The statement, "Pure religion and undefiled before God and the Father is this, To visit the fatherless and widows in their affliction and to keep himself unspotted from the world" (James 1:27) is an example of the concern of James. The book is packed with instructions which would help Christians to grow into maturity.

1 and 2 Peter

More than likely written after the outbreak of the Neronian persecutions in A. D. 64, 1 Peter could well be entitled "guidelines for triumphant living in trying times." Christians were undoubtedly disturbed by the growing persecutions they were enduring. Peter assured them that all believers have a security which cannot be shattered, whatever the trials faced. As pilgrims scattered in various parts of the earth, the followers of Christ are to live so "that God in all things may be glorified through Jesus Christ" (1 Peter 4:11). In citizenship obligations, even under a ruler like Nero, in vocational responsibilities, in marriage and every other relationship the motivation of Christians should be that of bearing a faithful witness.

Wives are advised to accept the headship of the husband in the home and to respect him in such a way "that, if any obey not the word, they also may without the word be won by the conversation of the wives; while they behold your chaste conversation coupled with fear" (1 Peter 3:1,2).

Through suffering and every other experience Christ is to be magnified and men are to be moved, despite their cynicism and hostility, to see by one's life the reality of one's Christian experience. "Having your conversation honest among the Gentiles: that, whereas they speak against you as evildoers, they may by your good words, which they shall behold, glorify God in the day of visitation" (1 Peter 2:12).

Two great missions themes stand out in 2 Peter. The first is the judgment foreseen for all the earth. God who did not spare angels from judgment will surely not spare men (2 Peter 2:4). The unrighteous face inevitable judgment (2 Peter 2:9). Even those who have had some Christian enlightenment but who have turned away for the attractions of the world also face the same end (2 Peter 2:20-22).

The second is one of the most heartwarming and inspiring assurances found anywhere in this epistle: "The Lord is not slack concerning his promise, as some men count slackness; but is longsuffering to us-ward, not willing that any should perish, but that all should come to repentance" (2 Peter 3:9). As all the Scriptures disclose concerning the outworking of the divine plan of redemption, God does not want men to be lost but goes to the uttermost, short of forcing their wills, to persuade everyone of his need of reconciliation with God. Yet even the promise of 2 Peter 3:9 is followed by a warning as well as another assurance: "But the day of the Lord will come as a thief in the night; in which the heavens shall pass away with a great noise, and the elements shall melt with fervent heat . . ." (2 Peter 3:10). All that belongs to the world of evil, having been judged, will perish; and a new heaven and a new earth are assured.

It is obvious that what is said here has implications for all men for all time. It therefore is vital to missionary concern.

1, 2, 3 John

Ephesus 90

From 1 John, especially, several emphases related to missions are deserving of consideration.

Anyone who denies his sin only deceives himself (1 John 1:8; 3:8).

Confession of sin leads to forgiveness. "If we confess our sins, he is faithful and just, and will forgive our sins and cleanse us from all unrighteousness" (1 John 3:9). This is a universal assurance.

The world and all its evil are destined to pass away. This prediction made elsewhere, especially in 2 Peter, is strongly affirmed here (1 John 2:16-17).

The way of deliverance from sin for all men is through a new birth. This comes from faith in Jesus Christ (1 John 4:9; 5:1).

Those who love God are bound to love one another (1 John 4:11). Hate is evidence that love of God does not exist in one's heart and makes his profession a lie (1 John 1:5-7).

Jude

The letter of Jude, like James, seems to have been written by a half-brother of our Lord, possibly around A.D. 80. By this time a great deal of false belief had crept into the organized church and was giving serious difficulty. It was enough to have to contend with hostile and pagan forces from without, but to resist the destructive effort of false teachers within was a trying test. This short letter, so vividly expressed, indicates how profoundly concerned its author was about the issues the church then faced. Thus it urges Christians to "contend for the faith which was once for all delivered to the saints" (Jude 1:3).

Gnostic

Jude saw the inevitable judgment which will come to false teachers, as it did to Israel in its spiritual backsliding and to Sodom and Gomorrah. The relevance of the letter to the church in this day is obvious. The false teaching of those who now assume the right to correct or deny the Scriptures is a grim problem to the church and a source of grave confusion for the world. They make all the more difficult a breakthrough of effective witness.

The one heartening realization that comes from a study of Jude is that the modern church is not the only one which has had to content with heresy. Jude, as well as a number of other epistles, discloses wickedness even in the early church. Yet the church had power then to overcome its problems. That same power is still available to those who meet its conditions.

Revelation

95 [handwritten annotation]

The book of Revelation cannot be understood unless it is remembered that it too was written in times of extreme persecution and heresy.

The seven churches addressed in the opening chapters of the book were products themselves of missionary witness. Careful study will disclose problems in practically all of these churches such as are well known today. The churches then as now needed nothing more than to repent and to return to their first love.

The book discloses many glorious assurances for the encouragement of the faithful. Their triumph would be certain. The blessings of the victorious church would be beyond imagination.

Several emphases in Revelation seem deeply relevant to missions.

Emphasis upon the ultimate universal worship of Christ. "And every creature which is in heaven, and on the earth, and under the earth, and such as are in the sea, and all that are in them, heard I saying, Blessing, and honour, and glory, and power, be unto him that sitteth upon the throne, and unto the Lamb for ever and ever," said John (Rev. 5:13).

Stress upon the fact that multitudes beyond number from every nation, tribe, people, and tongue will eventually stand before the throne of the Lamb in adoration of him. This uncountable host is representative of the product of worldwide witness for Christ. The multitudes who will respond to the missionary message are so numerous as "no man could number" (Rev. 7:9).

Focus upon the fact that the kingdoms of this earth will eventually become the kingdom of Christ, and he shall reign forever and ever (Rev. 11:15). Later John told us, "And I heard as it were the voice of a great multitude, and as the voice of many waters, and as the voice of mighty thunderings, saying, Alleluia: for the Lord God omnipotent reigneth" (Rev. 19:6). The Lamb of God, the Alpha and Omega, is now designated "King of kings and Lord of lords" (Rev. 19:16).

Emphasis on the coming judgment of all the earth. In passages such as Revelation 14:15-16; 18:1; and 20:12-15, the fact that becomes obvious that at last every man will appear before the throne of Christ; and there will follow a separation between those who have believed on him and those who have rejected him. The whole world and the whole race will be involved.

Emphasis on the eternal blessedness of the redeemed. Chapter 21 especially discloses, as does the last chapter of Isaiah (Isa. 66:22), a new heaven and a new earth yet to come. The blessedness of those who come to God through Christ is stated in the assurance that he "will wipe away every tear from their eyes, and death shall be no more, neither shall there be mourning nor crying nor pain anymore, for former things have passed away." This promise has been an undying source of comfort and assurance to multitudes across all the centuries. The glory of God is to be the light of this new city, in which the blessed dwell forever, and the Lamb is to be the "lamp." By this light shall the nations walk; and the kings of the earth shall bring their glory into the city.

Emphasis on the continuing and universal invitation that remains open to men even until the end of time. Almost at the close of the book of Revelation, and thus of the New Testament, stands the glorious statement: "And the spirit and the bride say, Come. And let him that heareth say, Come. And let him that is athirst come. And whosoever will, let him take the water of life freely" (Rev. 22:17).

The Holy Spirit continues his work in the world, inviting and persuading men, through every means consistent with divine character, to turn to God and be reconciled to him through Christ. The church, the "bride" of Christ, if faithfully fulfilling its mission, is always extending the invitation, Come. Everyone who hears is asked to share in the invitation and to invite others to join him. And, lest anyone should feel he is left out, the invitation is made universal: "Whosoever is athirst, let him come." This is the grand *crescendo* of the missionary message of the Bible. This is the divine guarantee, together with the cross and the empty tomb, validated also by God's work of changing men across all the centuries, that God "willeth not" any man should perish but that all should come unto him.

Requirements for Credit

This book is the text for course 3673 of subject area 36 (Missions) in the Christian Development Courses of the Church Study Course. If credit is desired for this course through class study or reading, the following requirements must be met:

I. Classwork

1. This course is designed for ten (10) or more hours of class study and carries four (4) credits for such usage. If the course is studied in a class setting of less than ten (10) hours, the following criteria apply:

(1) Seven and one half (7½) class hours—three (3) credits

(2) Five (5) class hours—two (2) credits

(3) Two and one half (2½) class hours—one (1) credit

The teacher will indicate the length of the class and the number of credits to be granted on Form 151, "Request for Course Credit."

2. The teacher should request credits for herself. A person who teaches a course for Youth or Adults (in any subject area) will be granted the same number of credits as class members.

3. The church training director, or the person designated by the church, should complete Form 151, "Request for Course Credit," and forward it after completion of the class to the Church Study Course Awards Office, 127 Ninth Avenue, North, Nashville, Tennessee 37234.

II. Reading Credit

1. A person may receive one credit toward the diploma on which he is working by reading this book.

2. Upon completion of the reading, he must complete Form 151, "Request for Course Credit," He should give the completed form to the church training director or to the person designated by his church to be responsible for administering the Church Study Course.

3. The church training director, or the person designated by the church, will see that the request is completed, signed, and forwarded to the Church Study Course Awards Office, 127 Ninth Avenue, North, Nashville, Tennessee 37234.

III. Awards and Records

Two copies of the course credit award form will be sent by the Church Study Course Awards Office to the church. The original copy should be filed in church training record and the duplicate given to the individual.